A NEW HEART

A
NEW
HEART

Selwyn Hughes

KINGSWAY PUBLICATIONS
EASTBOURNE

ISBN 0 86065 199 1

Unless otherwise indicated, Scripture quotations
are from the Authorized Version (crown copyright).

NIV = New International Version
© New York International Bible Society 1978

Front cover design by Vic Mitchell

Printed in Great Britain for
KINGSWAY PUBLICATIONS LTD
Lottbridge Drove, Eastbourne, E. Sussex BN23 6NT by
Richard Clay (The Chaucer Press) Ltd, Bungay, Suffolk.
Typesetting by Nuprint Services Ltd, Harpenden, Herts.

CONTENTS

PREFACE

In an age when great emphasis is being placed by Christian leaders on the need to evangelize, some consideration ought to be given to the fact that before we can successfully and effectively evangelize others, we ourselves must be fully evangelized.

The way in which Christ proceeds to fully evangelize the human heart, and bring it completely under his domain, is the main concern of this book.

It is my earnest prayer that those who read may experience, as did the two disciples on the road to Emmaus, the presence of the risen Christ, and say: 'Did not our hearts *glow* within us as he talked with us by the way' (Lk 24:32 Berkeley Version).

SELWYN HUGHES

1

A new heart

The gospel of Jesus Christ is a religion of *new* things. It offers to men a new birth, a new life, a new hope, a new joy and a new covenant. Such is the revolutionizing power of Christ's evangel, his good news, that when a man comes in contact with its force, he is never the same person again. He is, in fact, according to the Bible, a *new* creature. The gospel also promises its converts that when at last they lay down the cares and sorrows of this life, it is only to take up in eternity a new song and a new name.

However, out of all the fascinating new things which Christ offers his disciples, none is perhaps more intriguing than his offer of a new heart.

The promise is first given in the prophecy of Ezekiel, chapter 36, verse 26: 'A new heart will I give you and a new spirit will I put within you.' Someone has said in relation to the question of Christianity that the heart of the matter is simply the matter of the heart. How thrilling, therefore, is the triumphant declaration of the risen Christ who, in the book of Revelation, says, 'Behold, I make all things new' (21:5). By his eternal power he has been changing hearts for centuries, is doing it at the present moment and will go on doing it until the last second of recorded time.

Christ's offer of a new heart to men and women is, without doubt, one of the greatest promises of the Bible.

Its importance lies in a very simple fact—we so badly need it. 'The heart', said Jeremiah, 'is deceitful above all things and desperately wicked: who can know it?' (17:9). And Jesus had this to say: 'For out of the heart proceed evil thoughts, murders, adulteries, fornications, thefts, false witness, blasphemies' (Mt 15:19). If a sinner really wishes to understand his heart, 'then let him listen,' says Dr Oswald Chambers, 'to his own mouth in an unguarded frame for five minutes.' An unknown poet says:

> I know a bosom which within,
>   Contains the world's sad counterpart:
> 'Tis here—the reign of death and sin;
>   O God, evangelize my heart!

'Evangelize my heart!' What an exciting thought! Isn't this exactly what we need?

Assuredly it is! However, in what way can God answer such a prayer? We readily admit the effectiveness of evangelism that is carried on every week from the pulpit and by the men and women in the pews, for with such assistance God is bringing thousands to his fold. We know, too, that evangelism is intensely objective in its aims, for it seeks out not only men and women across the street but those across the sea. It flings its arms around the five continents and seeks to bring the whole world to God.

However, in our efforts to bring a dying world to Christ, have we forgotten that evangelism can be something else besides objective? It can be subjective too! Its quiet power can beat as effectively in the human heart as in the massed campaigns or large auditoriums where thousands gather to hear the word of life. In fact, the more God is allowed to evangelize the heart, the more effectively his influence can be spread through that heart to the world around. All evangelism requires the assistance of man, and given our consent and co-operation, there is no limit to what God can do. The Almighty respects the personality he has made and he will never try to advance his cause by violating the nature he has created.

'Given our consent and co-operation'—this is the hinge upon which the whole thing hangs. So often we overlook it. We talk in glowing terms about objective evangelism with its planned campaigns and strategic advances into the enemy's territory, but before we set out to win men and women for God, ought we not to ask ourselves this question: How much of a grip has God got upon me? The secret of all evangelism, whether objective or subjective, lies in a very simple truth; it requires the obedience and surrender of man to make it possible.

In these pages we shall be thinking together of the various ways in which God undertakes to evangelize not so much the world but the individual human heart. How does he set about it? What is the first thing he proceeds to do in order to overcome the problem of sin in a person's life?

The answer lies here: he does it by giving a new heart!

If the gospel of Jesus Christ does not make us anew then it fails to meet human need. The best it can do otherwise is to cover our unregenerate nature with a veneer of respectable religion. It merely sugar-coats the rottenness and veils the real nature of our disease. In all our hearts lies the virus of sin, and if we are to be rescued from its power then only God can help us. Some account for the presence of sin in the heart in different ways. It is called an 'evolutionary legacy', 'the moral hangover from our animal ancestry' or 'merely the growing pains of the human race'. However, the only real explanation of sin's presence in the heart is given in the Bible. Sin began in the heart of one of heaven's dignitaries who, lifted up by pride, rebelled and revolted against God and, as a result, was cast out of heaven. It was through the temptation of this fallen being—Satan—that our first parents fell into sin, and as a consequence of their disobedience, sin has remained in human hearts ever since.

The Bible treats sin as something more than theological fiction or a pathological state; it shows its dreadful power, a power from which an omnipotent God can only save us by the gift of his Son dying on the cross as a substitute for sin. Sin has played havoc with God's fair earth, and the effect we see around us in the world outside is also experienced in the human heart. The world within is as warped as the world without, and salvation is the thrilling discovery that God does something more with sin than ignore it: he has found a way to forgive. Sin is not a mere social problem; it is intensely *personal*. He who died for the whole world died for everyone in it.

When God changes the heart it means much more than reinforcing it with new desires. It means much more also than mere medication, injection or even transfusion. According to the Bible, God does not attempt to mend the heart, but takes away the old that he might replace it with the new. When a man is converted, therefore, he receives, as the Bible promises, a *new* heart!

What, then, are the characteristics of such a heart?

There are, of course, many and we can only consider a few of them in detail. Before we do so, let it be said that the moment a man becomes a Christian, he is a 'new creature'—a revolutionary change takes place. The transformation usually becomes evident to himself immediately and to others gradually. In his new heart he is conscious that things which once troubled him are no longer there, and things about which he had no concern now occupy his mind and thoughts to a great degree.

Instead of selfishness, there is selflessness

There is nothing more elemental in human nature before the new birth than self-interest and self-concern. Some are not even ashamed to own up to it. They will tell you without a blush that the only thing they live for is to make money and get on, ignoring everything and everyone who may stand in their path. Others, not so open, point out that their aims are to serve humanity and make the world a better place when they leave it than when they entered it. However, deep down in every unregenerate heart there is a fundamental desire to serve one's own ends and to pursue, avowedly or not, aims that merely end with self.

When, however, the radical revolution of the new birth takes place, and a new heart is given by Christ, a surprising discovery is made. The heart is no longer taken up with self, but with Christ. The reason for this, of course, is that Christ sets himself up in the midst of the new heart, and, to quote Henry Scougal, 'diffuseth Himself through all their faculties'. Scougal goes on to say, too, speaking of those to whom this great change has taken place, 'He animates them with his life and Spirit that they may have no will or affections of their own, no desires or inclinations different from His, but that every pulse may answer the motions of His heart, and all their powers be actuated and enlivened by His Spirit.'

This, then, is the crux of the whole matter. It is impossible to act like Christ until we first receive him, and having received him, he abides in the heart to make such a change effective. The apostle Paul discovered after his conversion that he no longer wished to carve a career for himself in law, but was quite content to become 'less than the least of all the saints'. John the Baptist, at the height of his popularity, suddenly came face to face with Jesus, and although he was the most talked about person of his day, he was quite happy to become a nonentity so that Christ might become known. He became an utterly selfless man and cried, 'He must increase and I must decrease.' D. L. Moody was one of the greatest evangelists of his day, and when the world was ringing with his name, F. B. Meyer, who knew him well, had this to say, 'It seemed when I talked to him about his success that he had never heard of himself.' The reason, of course, was that Moody was no longer concerned about himself; he was more interested in what men thought of Jesus Christ.

There are some who strive by human effort to become selfless men. They set out on a path that leads to self-discipline and altruism, and spend their lives in the service of others. The question is often asked, therefore: Will God dwell in such a heart? The answer is, 'No!' God will only dwell in a heart that has accepted him, and whatever principles guide a man who does not know Christ, you can be sure that deep down in that heart, though perhaps camouflaged and concealed, lies self-interest and self-concern. This basic bias might not easily be seen but it is there nevertheless, for the root of all sin is selfishness. William Law remarked, 'A Christ not in us is a Christ not ours.' In order for us to live like Christ and to reflect his grace and love to all around, it is necessary for us to receive him. When he comes in, self is crossed out, and the heart which holds him lives no longer for itself, but for the Lord.

Instead of weakness, there is authority

The question is often asked of Christians: How is it possible to live a righteous life in a world where temptation is so strong? There are many Christians who will tell you that they are frankly amazed at their own ability to stand amidst all the seductions and allurements of a sinful world. What is it then that holds the Christian's heart so firm and fast amid the flux and flow of life?

It is the fact that the presence of Jesus Christ in the heart buttresses and reinforces the life against the power of temptation. With Christ in the heart, a Christian need no longer fear the things that once shook him to the depth of his soul. It is more than a question of a *strong* will; it is more the question of a *surrendered* will. When the Son of God occupies the mind, his presence affects every area of thought. It strengthens, enriches and makes all things new.

What a sense of security manifests itself in the heart of a man who realizes that his life is governed by the Master. As he moves through life hand in hand with Christ, he develops a sense of moral authority that marks him out among others. It is the presence of Christ in the heart that has made men down the ages invincible. John Knox was no stronger by nature than any of the other men of his day, yet with Christ within, he was bold enough to denounce Mary, Queen of Scots, in such terms that made her shake with terror. When you take up your New Testament and examine it carefully, you will find that the disciples moved through Jerusalem, after Pentecost, with far more daring than they had done when Christ was with them on earth. The boldness and courage which distinguished them in the Acts of the Apostles stemmed from this living fact—Christ was not merely with them, but *within* them. They were conscious as they spoke that behind them lay all the authority of the Royal Throne. When Paul wrote to the Corinthian converts, rebuking them for their irregularities, he was careful at one point in his letter to pass on his opinion as a private individual. The words he wrote there seem to carry little emphasis as compared to the passages he uttered as the mouthpiece of the Lord. When he wrote, 'I command, yet not I but the Lord,' he possessed a power and an authority otherwise lacking.

What it amounts to is this: only Christ, ruling and reigning in the heart, can give it moral authority and spiritual stability. The Psalmist talks about the heart being 'established' and, indeed, this characteristic is present in every heart that knows the Lord.

Instead of falsity, there is loyalty

Tennyson in one of his poems speaks about 'being loyal to the royal in oneself'. If you were to ask many people, they would regard this as a good and acceptable definition of the Christian life. However, the truth is that when a man receives Christ, he is no longer concerned about 'being loyal to the royal' in himself; he is more concerned about 'being loyal to the royal' in Jesus.

I once heard a man witness to his change of heart, and one of the things he said has always remained with me. 'Before I was converted,' he said, 'I was a church member who did my best to work up religious enthusiasm. I used to go through life trying all the time to remember I was a member of a certain church, and that my life and actions should be in accordance with its reputation. However, more often than not, I would forget my relationship to that church when some other interest would engage my attention. Then one day I received Christ and, after that, it was no longer a church member relationship but attachment to a living Person: and that made all the difference.'

It does make all the difference. Loyalty to the living Christ enables a man to move through the world with a sense of true dedication. A person who tries to attach himself to Christ, without the great change taking place, will find that when it comes to a decision between natural interests and divine, the natural will win. Selfish interests are far more dominant in an unregenerated heart than any others, but when Christ comes in, he inspires such devotion that loyalty to him streams out of the heart.

When Sir Wilfred Grenfell first heard D. L. Moody preach, he was so impressed that he left this on record: 'He left a new idea in my mind, the idea that loyalty to a living leader was religion.' Real Christians are people who are so captivated by Christ that there is no room for anyone else but him and his principles. When the heart is taken up with Christ then it is not difficult to understand why no other loyalty can creep into the soul. Such a heart knows the very crux of vital Christian living.

Hence we have deep reason to be glad that God offers to all men a new heart. Reformation may change a man's habits but only God can change his heart. Christianity means much more than commemorating the death of Jesus Christ; it is vital contact with him day by day.

The new heart is Christ's palace. On its throne he lives and rules. Given control, by our consent and co-operation, there is no limit to the change he makes, and which he can to make, day by day.

2

A heart that feels for all

In Paul's second letter to the Corinthians chapter
11, he uses these remarkable words: 'O ye

2

A heart that feels for all

In Paul's second letter to the Corinthians chapter 6, verse 11, he uses these remarkable words: 'O ye Corinthians, our mouth is open unto you, our heart is enlarged.' Again and again, in John Wesley's Journal, one comes across an entry like this: 'Preached with great enlargement of heart.' And it is said of George Whitefield that when, during the revival of the eighteenth century, he addressed the miners of Bristol, whose black faces were stained with veins of white as the tears coursed down their cheeks, he cried, 'O men of Bristol, my heart is enlarged toward you.' The Psalmist prays thus in the Old Testament, 'I will run the way of thy commandments, when thou shalt enlarge my heart' (Ps 119:32).

When you comb the record of Christ's days upon earth, you find that there was never anyone with a heart so large as his. As he moves across Palestine he has time and concern for everyone he meets. Nothing can hurry him past a seeking soul, and whether, like Peter, they smell of the sea, or like the woman at the well they bear the name of a harlot, Jesus Christ has room in his heart for them all. In the Praetorium his thoughts are so taken up with others that he even discusses with Pilate his mission to the world. On his way to Golgotha, he turns to the weeping women and says, 'Weep not for me, but rather for yourselves and for your children.' On the cross he prays for the brutes taken up with Christ then it is not difficult to understand why no other loyalty can creep into the soul. Such a heart knows the very crux of vital Christian living.

Hence we have deep reason to be glad that God offers to all men a new heart. Reformation may change a man's habits but only God can change his heart. Christianity means much more than commemorating the death of Jesus Christ; it is vital contact with him day by day.

The new heart is Christ's palace. On its throne he lives and rules. Given control, by our consent and co-operation, there is no limit to the change he makes, and which he can continue to make, day by day.

who murdered him and asks that they may be forgiven.

It would not be difficult either to make a list of Christ's followers who have found room in their hearts for the multitudes. There have been many who in this love-hungry world have tried to:

> Raise the fallen, cheer the faint.
> Heal the sick and lead the blind.

One of the names that ranks high on the list of those who have cared for others is that of Catherine Booth. She was never well. When she was fourteen years of age, her physical weakness resulted in a curvature of the spine. She was forced to spend a long time upon her back. Later her lungs became affected and she contracted tuberculosis. Before she died she endured two whole years of terrible pain and would never agree to her doctor administering a pain-numbing drug. Yet, despite her acute discomfort, she never complained. The doctor who attended her was an agnostic and she felt more concern for him than she did for herself. She longed to win him to Christ and after her death the doctor is reported to have said, 'Her courage and anxiety for my welfare was beautiful.'

Yet, if we were honest, we would admit that not all Christians have this concern for folk. Most are so taken up with their own problems that they have little time to consider the plight of others. They have no urge to save like the poet who cried:

> Then with a rush the intolerable craving
> Shivers through me like a trumpet call.
> Oh to save these! to perish for their saving,
> Die for their life, be offered for them all.

Let me put it to you now: Have you a heart that feels for all? Is your heart like the apostle Paul's, large enough to take in others? Perhaps you feel that although you have no 'ache' to save, you long to know something of this compassion for others. The way God enlarges the Christian's heart is what we shall be concerned with here, and he does it in many ways.

He does it by giving us a great love for all humanity

So many of us spend our lives in compartments. We move among people of our own social status. We talk most freely with those who are our equals, and more often than not, we resent the company of those we consider beneath us in dignity, education and background. Love is the only answer. Such love, of course, is a gift, but it is freely given in answer to importunate prayer. Christ is able to bring into our lives a stream of love for the lost which, although it doesn't solve all problems, provides us with the power to keep on loving even when our affection is met with scorn. It is almost impossible to love a drunkard who lies in the gutter and wallows in his pitiable condition; the natural reaction is to turn away in disgust. However, such is the love that the Lord plants in our hearts when we ask him that there is no situation we will ever face that cannot be answered by love.

One of the witnesses borne to Christ in *The Letters of James Smethan* is this: 'Christ takes your view of things and mentions no other. He takes the old woman's view of things and shows a great interest in wash powder; Isaac Newton's view of things and wings among the stars with him; the artist's view of things and feeds the lilies; the lawyer's and shares the justice of things. But He never plays the lawyer or the philosopher or the artist to the old woman. He is above the littleness.'

In other words, Jesus was adept at meeting all people on their own level. His skill in meeting people and talking to them about the things in which they were most interested is seen at its best in the story of the woman at the well. When Christ met this loose woman, he did not suddenly take on an air of spiritual pre-eminence and give her a lecture on chastity. He said simply, 'Would you please give me a drink of water?' In that one simple question, he made the first step toward that woman's heart.

The love that Christ gives to his disciples is not a love that runs on lines of mere affinity. It loves even those who are unlovely. It shows itself in many ways. It can make a man in his sixties, as Dr Sangster tells us in his book *Let Me Commend*, 'take up guinea pigs in order that he might tunnel his way into the heart of a boy.' It can lead a man like Norman Macleod to stand in the smoke of a smithy chatting in friendly fashion to the farrier, and of this the latter confessed, 'He never came into my shop without talking to me as if he had been a blacksmith all his life.' It led Edward Irving, that great soulwinner, to call on a Glasgow cobbler because his own father had been a tanner, and through this he was able to develop a contact that led into the man's soul.

Another way in which God expands the heart is this:

He does it by showing us what people really need

Bishop Taylor Smith, during the 1914–18 war, was Chaplain General to His Majesty's Forces. During his term of office, a clergyman approached him and asked that he might be given a chaplaincy. Instead of giving a direct reply, the Bishop looked at his applicant, pulled out his pocket watch, and said, 'I am a soldier dying on the battlefield and I have three minutes to live—what have you to say to me?' Utterly taken aback, the man had nothing to say, and because he had no message for a dying man, his appeal was naturally dismissed.

If all life was suddenly reduced to three minutes, it would be easy then to see what people most needed.

There would be hardly any doubt in any Christian's mind. It could be summed up in one word—Christ! Because life goes on and we do not know when eternity will call us, it does not mean that people's needs are different. Christ is still the greatest need of all men who do not know him, and when we draw close to Christ's heart, this single fact is brought more closely into focus.

When Peter and the rest of the disciples stepped out of the Upper Room on the Day of Pentecost, they had been given an insight into the beating heart of Christ. They saw people as he saw them, and they knew it was Christ that men and women needed most. So instantly they set about telling them that this was their greatest need. 'They ceased not,' says the writer of the Acts of the Apostles, 'to teach and preach Jesus Christ.' When Saul of Tarsus met Jesus on the road to Damascus his whole life was changed. He suddenly realized that what the world needed was an experiential knowledge of the Son of God. Here is the record as it is set down in the Acts of the Apostles, '*Straightway* he preached Christ in the synagogues.'

It cannot be too strongly stressed that when Christ's disciples get near to his heart, they are instantly taken up with the fact that all men need to know him more than anything else in life. Paul, after his conversion (as we saw earlier), was no longer concerned with pursuing a career in law or politics. He lived to tell others of Jesus Christ.

Most people attempt to conceal their real need. Some do it deliberately; others are unaware of what their greatest need really is. When a Christian is in living touch with Christ, he finds that the introduction of Christ to others becomes natural and easy. In dealing with others you will be more concerned with presenting Christ than theological controversy, and from your own burning heart you will see men for what they really are—sheep without a shepherd.

He does it by providing the power that makes for effective soulwinning

No one can expect much success in reaching men and women unless he has been filled with the power that makes it possible. This power is promised by Christ in the New Testament, and is, in fact, the greatest prerequisite in producing an enlarged heart. Look how it operated in the lives of the disciples. Before they were filled with this power they were like frightened sheep in a pen, sitting in the Upper Room in Jerusalem for fear of the Jews. Then suddenly there burst into the room the supernatural power of the Holy Spirit that fired them with a holy zeal, and instantly they were men transformed. No longer were they afraid of people's opinions. In fact, after Pentecost, they were the ones that shaped public opinion and, by their words and deeds, did much to change the trends of their day and generation.

When you look at the lives of the disciples before Pentecost, you cannot help but be struck by the fact that they had very little interest in reaching the multitudes. When Christ was with them, leading, directing and encouraging, they were usually ready to obey his commands, but when he left them, even though only for a while, they quarrelled, argued and debated hotly among themselves concerning such things as position and prestige. While Christ was on the Mount of Transfiguration, for example, some of them struggled in prayer over a demon-possessed boy in the valley, but without success. All this, however, is reversed at Pentecost. The power of the Holy Spirit flows into them and seems to carry its own built-in compassion. At once they set out to reach the multitudes; their hearts were enlarged to take in not only Jerusalem, but the whole world.

There is something about the power of the Holy Spirit that, once he invades our lives, gives our hearts an upheaval. He turns half-hearted Christians into flames of fire. If you have not got this great compassion that Christ gives, then seek to be filled with his power. Make this your prayer and heaven will answer:

I want, dear Lord, a love that feels for all.
　A deep, strong love that answers every call.
A love like Thine, a love divine, a love for
　high and low.
On me, dear Lord, a love like this bestow.

3

A heart from sin set free

Most Christians believe in the biblical truth of holiness but, for many, their conception of it is so vague and nebulous that it lies most of the time in a dark shadow. Those who are clear about their beliefs differ greatly concerning the method by which holiness becomes a reality. To some it is a crisis as real and positive as conversion; to others it is a process of gradual achievement that goes on day by day.

Great controversy has raged around the teaching of New Testament holiness in almost every decade of the Christian church. Those who see sin as having made deep inroads into human nature say that the only thing God can do with sin is forgive it. Others see the soul as a battleground on which a long drawn out guerrilla warfare takes place between the flesh and the Spirit. And there are those who claim, as did John Wesley, that holiness can be imparted by a sudden influx of divine grace.

Which of these theories is true? Can Christ effect in a Christian's heart a perfect or a partial cure over the disease of sin? Is he only able to repress it or can he remove it from the heart? Will he answer such a prayer as Charles Wesley's when he cried: 'Take away the love of sinning'? These are the questions which occupy us in this chapter.

Thoughtful Christians have often been disturbed by the fact that long after conversion and the experience of forgiveness of sin, they are still conscious of sin in their lives. Paul, speaking (so I believe) *subsequent* to his conversion, felt that another 'self' dwelt within him (Rom 7:21). The famous Launcelot Andrews once confessed long after his conversion, 'I am made of sin.' William Law, a great thinker and a great Christian of the eighteenth century, remarked, 'I am a dead dog.' Alexander Whyte, one of the saintliest men to come out of Scotland, described himself on one occasion as 'the worst man in Edinburgh'. These are not the words of young Christians but ripe saints. They are not to be dismissed as pious hyperbole either; they are the words of honest men. 'In my younger days,' wrote Richard Baxter, 'my concern was mostly about my actual thought, word or action. But now I am much more troubled about the inward defects and omissions . . . the want of vital virtues or graces in the soul.'

The conclusion may be drawn by some: if such saints of God felt that way then what hope is there for me in my personal quest after holiness? Take heart, for there are multitudes of Christians, past and present, who claim to have experienced divine destruction of sin in their lives, and although they would never claim that sin has been eradicated from their hearts, they testify to an inner cleansing that for them was the difference between defeat and victory. They cried with the hymnist:

> I want, dear Lord, a heart that's true and clean.
> A sunlit heart, with not a cloud between.
> A heart like thine, a heart divine, a heart as white as snow.
> On me, dear Lord, a heart like this bestow.

And just as God answered their prayer—he can answer yours too!

As you read carefully the lives of great Christians of the past, you will find that, generally speaking, they divide into two classes. There are those (like the ones we quoted above) who speak often of the consciousness of sin within them, and there are others who testify to God entirely cleansing their hearts from sin, 'slaying the dire root and seed of it', after which they enter into an experience that is like being in the foyer of heaven.

Consider Commissioner S. L. Brengle of the Salvation Army, for example, speaking of the great experience when God sanctified his soul. He says, 'On January 9th 1885, at about nine o'clock in the morning, God sanctified my soul. I was in my own room at the time but in a few moments I went out and met a man and told him what God had done for me. Two mornings after that, just as I got out of bed and was reading some words of Jesus, He gave me such a blessing as I never dreamed a man could have this side of heaven. I walked out over Boston Common before breakfast weeping for joy and praising God. Oh, how I loved! I loved the sparrows. I loved the dogs. I loved the strangers who hurried past me. I loved the heathen. I loved the world.' He went on, 'Do you want to know what holiness is? It is love...love that brings one into perfect and unbroken sympathy with the Lord Jesus in His toil and travail to bring a lost and rebel world back to God.'

We find similar statements made by other great Christians—Hudson Taylor, Thomas Cook, Frances Ridley Havergal, to name but a few. All are on record as claiming a similar experience to Commissioner Brengle's. John Wesley, although he never testified to having experienced what I am now describing, taught his followers that sanctification is wrought in the soul in an instant by an act of God in response to an act of faith. However, it is to the apostle Paul that we owe the greatest debt for illumination on this subject. In Romans chapter 5, Paul describes sin as dominating a sinner's life; it reigns over him and within him and, despite his great efforts, it simply cannot be

broken. In Romans chapter 7, Paul describes the power of
sin that was still within him even after he had become a
Christian. If it be asked: how do we know that Paul was a
Christian when he stated this, then let this answer suffice.
In Romans 7:22, Paul says, 'I delight in the law of God
after the inward man.' It is my view that no sinner could
possibly delight in God's law when he is in an unregenerated and unconverted state. I believe Paul was speaking
here of his experience *after* conversion, and conscious still
of indwelling sin.

There are three main groupings in the Christian church
in connection with the matter of New Testament holiness
and they can be generally classified in the following order:

—those who believe holiness is imputed
—those who believe holiness is imparted
—those who believe holiness is developed.

Permit me to bring each of these more clearly into
focus. Those who believe that holiness is imputed say that
because man is a dyed-in-the-wool sinner, the idea that he
can really be holy is an illusion. Man is a sinner, they
assert, and will always be a sinner. There is sin not only in
his vices but in his virtues too. God, however, flings
around such sinners, at the moment they repent of their
sin, the robe of Christ's righteousness, imputing to them a
righteousness they cannot acquire by any other means.
When this takes place then God sees them for ever after in
the spotless garments of his Son. The emphasis of these
thinkers is that righteousness can neither be achieved nor
received in this life. Our righteousness is in him and in him
alone. No one can deny, of course, that the imputation of
righteousness is taught in the Scriptures. It is when the
emphasis is placed disproportionately upon it that problems arise.

Those who believe that holiness is imparted claim that

there is an experience awaiting all believers by which purity can be imparted in a crisis experience, almost by a stroke of omnipotence. The belief received great prominence under John Wesley. He taught that there were two distinct stages in the Christian experience, the first consisting of justification and the second, sanctification. In sanctification, God entirely cleanses the heart from sin, and the Christian is then able to enter into a life of great victory and power. Wesley claimed that though a man was 'entirely sanctified', he was still subject to ignorance, mistakes, infirmities, but no longer to guilt. Wesley's brother, Charles, summed up the belief and longing of all who share this view:

> He wills that I should holy be.
> That holiness I long to feel,
> That full divine conformity
> To all my Saviour's righteous will.

The third group, those who believe that holiness is developed, see the work of God in the soul proceeding along the lines of a slow but steady improvement. Although they recognize the truth of imputation, they do not lay the stress there. One theologian suggests that this might be because legal metaphors do not greatly appeal to those who hold to this view of holiness. They prefer to think not so much in terms of how God *sees* man as holy but how God may *make* him holy. Many of them would agree to an element of truth in Wesley's teaching, that a sudden moment of vision or a special occasion of spiritual receptivity can bring about a mighty experience in the soul, but they would argue that life brings many moments of vision and it would be wrong to select just one experience and lay claim to that as unique. God is constantly at work in the soul, they argue, and although there are times of crisis, the fallow periods are important too. In the steady day after day plodding, the work of God is done. Their conclusion is that we *grow* in holiness not enter into it.

My conclusion is that holiness is both imputed and imparted, and then worked out in the daily issues of life. Whatever our view, every Christian must recognize the obligation of holiness, and that God's one intolerance is sin. We must all bow before the majestic admonition: 'Be ye holy for I am holy.'

Here, perhaps, we ought to pause to clarify two important Bible words: salvation and sanctification. The word *salvation* is a word with no sharp edges. It is a great and wonderful biblical word but it takes its meaning from its context. It can be used in connection with being saved from sin's penalty at conversion. It can also be used in connection wth being saved from sin's power by a subsequent experience of the Spirit (sanctification) or it can be used to describe the future experience awaiting the Christian in heaven when he will be delivered from sin's presence. The word *salvation,* therefore, often embraces three great biblical truths: namely, Justification, Sanctification and Glorification.

Our purpose here is to relate the word *salvation* simply to the experience known as conversion, that moment when a soul passes from death into life or, as the Bible puts it, is 'born again'. When a person becomes a Christian, a new life from God is imparted to him and he is born of the Spirit. God's seed is deposited within him and, as a result, he does not deliberately practise sin (1 Jn 3:9). Any person who is truly 'born again' begins, in a sense, a completely new life. He stands in a new relationship to God, 'accepted in the beloved' (Eph 1:6), and is indwelt by the Holy Spirit (Rom 8:9). The Spirit of Christ and the Holy Spirit, by the way, are synonymous terms. This can be clearly seen from a comparison of the following Scriptures: 1 Peter 1:11 and 2 Peter 1:21.

Sanctification is a word with different shades of meaning. In the Old Testament the word is used in four senses. In Genesis 2:3, it means to be set apart—separation. In Exodus 13:12, it means to be given to—dedication. In Exodus 19:14, it means to be cleansed—purification. In Exodus 28:41, it means to be used—ministration. The word sanctification in the New Testament has a similar flavour. It is used to describe separation (1 Cor 1:2), dedication (2 Tim 2:21), purification (Eph 5:26) and ministration (Acts 20:32).

Because the word is so varied in meaning it has given rise to many differing interpretations. Some say sanctification is a process—a truth, of course, which cannot be denied. However, it can also be a crisis, as I shall endeavour to show. Wesley, in teaching sanctification as a crisis experience, always conceded that there was a growth before and afterwards, and borrowed an analogy from birth and death to clarify the issue. 'There is growth in the womb before birth,' he said, 'and a longer growth after. But birth can be both dated and timed. A man may be dying for months but when he breathes his last, he breathes it in an instant of time.'

If then sanctification is both a growth and a crisis, how does one proceed to enter into the crisis period? Permit me to share with you my own personal experience in this connection.

Following my conversion in my mid teens I came under the influence of some Christian friends who assured me that the next stage in my experience was to seek what they described as the 'baptism in the Spirit'. Having little knowledge of the Scriptures at that time, it was explained to me that I needed supernatural power in my life to witness for Jesus Christ and at the baptism in the Spirit, this would be given to me. It was an experience, I was told, in which I would be immersed in the power of the Spirit by the Lord Jesus Christ, and I would be turned upside down and inside out. And this actually happened.

One night I prayed that God would baptize me in the Spirit, that he would supply me with the power I so badly needed. In my case, I should explain, power meant a great deal to me for I was an extremely shy, timid, hesitant, uncommunicative teenager. As I prayed for this experience to take place, I wondered to myself: will I really be given enough power to break my inhibitions and turn me from a reticent follower of Christ into a fearless and flaming disciple?

Suddenly I was enveloped in the most beautiful and awesome experience. I felt as if thousands of volts of electricity were thudding into my personality. When it was over (about an hour later) I discovered that what my friends had told me was true—I was a new man. Fear and trepidation had vanished. On my way home from the service where this happened I talked freely to people about Jesus Christ—something that I was previously afraid of doing. The next morning being Sunday, I stepped out on to the street of the village where I lived and preached for about fifteen minutes in an open air service at which scores of people gathered. They were utterly amazed that the shy, young teenager they all knew could suddenly hold their attention with the story of his conversion. At work the next day, I found no difficulty whatsoever in witnessing to my workmates about Jesus Christ. They, too, couldn't get over the fact that my shyness had dissolved.

It was true: the baptism in the Spirit that my friends had told me about did turn me upside down and inside out! I was afraid of no one and began to preach the Gospel everywhere I could—on the streets, in trains and buses and sometimes, when invited, in the pulpits of different churches.

About six months later, I began to reflect on the fact that although I was experiencing a tremendous degree of power in my life, enabling me to witness for Jesus Christ, I was deeply troubled by sinful forces which, from time to time, stirred deep within me. I fought hard with such things as lust, sensuality, rebellion and other things, until one night, worn down by the conflict that was going on inside me, I shut myself in my room and prayed, 'Lord, inside me is a team of wild horses that are out of control. If you can't control them, no one can. And if they can't be controlled, then I would rather die.' I was rather desperate, as you can imagine from that prayer, but that night God met with me in an unforgettable way.

After several hours of waiting before God in prayer, I was given a vision of Christ upon the cross. I saw him hanging there, and even now as I write, I am conscious that the details of that vision were ineffaceably imprinted on my memory. I saw the blood flow out from his wounded side. I saw the spittle of the soldier upon his cheek. I saw his body writhe under the pain. Then suddenly the vision of Christ vanished, and all that remained was an empty cross. The Holy Spirit said to me, 'Now you step on the cross.'

As I pondered the meaning of this strange request, some words lodged themselves in my mind, words I had often read in the Bible but which now came home to me with a new illuminated meaning. They were these: 'I am crucified with Christ: nevertheless I live; yet not I, But Christ liveth in me' (Gal 2:20). Just days prior to this experience I had been reading a book by Dr Daniel Steele entitled *Milestone Papers* in which he said, 'When we come to consider the work of sanctification and purification in the believer's soul by the power of the Holy Spirit, we find that the aorist tense is consistently used. The tense, according to New Testament scholars, never indicates a continuous or repeated act but one which is momentary and done once and for all.' He had spoken particularly of the text that was now in my mind, and I remembered how he had expounded Paul's statement, 'I

am crucified,' as being a solemn definite act. The Holy
Spirit bore home to me at that moment that just as Christ
was placed upon a cross and had his life ended by
crucifixion, so now I, too, was invited to enter into a
similar experience. It occurred to me, as the vision stayed
before me, that there was no way I could atone for my
own sin as that had been fully and finally settled by Christ
on my behalf. This invitation of the Spirit was to place
myself symbolically in his hands so that a deathblow could
be delivered to the sinful tendencies that had so deeply
troubled me. In my vision I saw myself nailed to that
cross. There was no pain, just a consciousness of absolute
surrender. When the vision vanished, I was filled with a
deep and wonderful peace. I spent the whole night in
prayer, and the next day, even though I had foregone a
night's sleep, I felt as if I was walking on air. Over the days
and weeks that followed, I became aware that as my
previous encounter with the Holy Spirit had given me a
new sense of *power,* this had given me a new sense of
purity.

When sharing this experience with others, those of the
Pentecostal persuasion say that I received the baptism in
the Holy Spirit when I received *power.* Those of the
holiness persuasion say I received it when I experienced
purity. The older I grow, the more I see that the Holy
Spirit cannot be put on railway lines, so to speak, and run
only on the tracks of our preconceived ideas. My own
opinion of what I experienced in the light of Scripture is
that they were both genuine encounters with the Holy
Spirit. And what happened to me may not necessarily
take place in the same way in the lives of other Christians.
Some appear to enter the Christian life and receive
everything all at once. They are saved, empowered with
the Holy Spirit, and go on to show evidences of God's
purity in their lives in just a matter of weeks following
their conversion. Others, like myself, move a little more

slowly through the stages. In offering the testimony of my own experience I do so not that you might emulate it but that you might consider what I say, and see if it accords with the way God is leading you, and your understanding of the Scriptures.

What practical benefits did I gain from this experience of sanctification? It did not result, I found, in placing me beyond the possibility of a carnal thought, a stab of pride, a trace of envy. It meant rather that I became more conscious of the Holy Spirit's presence in my subconscious than I did of sin's presence. Evil was not eradicated in me (as some proponents of 'imparted holiness' believe) but I found that the eagerness for it had gone, the appetite for it brought under control and the hunger for it no longer a clamour. It wasn't that I found it impossible to sin—that would be going too far—I discovered, however, that it was possible not to sin. Temptation was still present in my life (indeed there is no ground to suppose that in this life we will ever pass beyond the range of temptation) but I found that I fought it with greater ease than before, and although at times there were struggles, fierce struggles, I sensed that something had happened inside me that, while not taking away my responsibility to say a flat 'no' to sin, reinforced my desire for God, bringing me out, time and time again, into complete and total victory. I was able swiftly to assess wrong thoughts in the light of the Spirit's presence in my heart, and seeing them to be evil, renounce them quickly and dismiss them as undeserving of even momentary attention. Now, close on forty years later, I look back on that experience with feelings of deep gratitude to God, and I will never cease to thank him for the day when, through the Holy Spirit's operation on my life, I felt his cooling, cleansing touch.

The question must now be faced: allowing for the fact that sanctification can be a crisis experience, what exactly happens in the life of a believer when this takes place? I believe myself that much of the work is done in the subconscious. Modern psychology tells us that down in the subconscious lie the instincts holding within them the race habits and tendencies. These instincts have gathered up within themselves the race experience which goes all the way back to Adam. They, therefore, have certain leanings, certain drives, which, unrestrained, tend toward evil. In conversion, there is a sweeping out of the conscious mind all that conflicts with the love of Christ and the establishing of his reign there. For weeks after conversion perhaps no conflict ensues, the new life reigns supreme. The instincts of the subconscious are cowed, so to speak, cowed but not converted. They soon demand recognition and expression. They knock at the door of the conscious. The supposed instincts are, as Dr E. Stanley Jones described them, 'like Chinese pirates who hide in the hold of a vessel and then rise up while the ship is on her voyage to try and capture the bridge and with it the ship. A fight ensues.' The issue, then, is this: can the subconscious be converted? Converted, yes. Eradicated, no.

Dr Leslie Weatherhead in his book *Psychology and Life* says, 'The instinctive forces cannot, by any known process, be eradicated and the method of evasion and pretence simply means that these forces function at the depth of the personality at which they cannot be controlled.' Many have tried to eradicate these instincts, but put out of the door, they come back through the window. 'In India,' says a famous missionary, 'I saw naked Sadhus, who had renounced the world and themselves, get very touchy about getting a proper place in the procession of people going to bathe in the Ganges. Their supposedly eradicated instincts showed through.' They cannot be eradicated.

Nor can they be repressed. If they are repressed then they are driven below and form what is called a complex. A complex is a 'system of emotionally toned ideas ranging around one central idea'. It is a festering point, like a boil, if you like, in the subconscious. Psychology says that the instincts can be sublimated—that is, turned into expression in a higher form. In other words, they can be converted. We cannot put them out nor can we put them under. In sanctifying them, God takes our former enemies and makes them our allies. The wild horses are tamed and harnessed to the tasks of the kingdom.

How then is this achieved? The answer is self-surrender. But, you say, didn't I do that at conversion? Yes, you did, in a measure but perhaps not wholly. Now, as you can see, there are deeper depths to be surrendered. The conscious mind became his at conversion, but the subconscious, the centre of divisions and inner clashes, must be laid at his feet as well. The self must be crucified in order to rise again. And the self is usually the last thing we are willing to give up. The missionary gives up home, friends, and family to go to another land; he gives up everything except himself. Thus he finds his inner self touchy over such things as position, place and power. The minister sacrifices a good deal to go into the ministry—everything except the minister. He finds himself preaching the gospel with a good deal of vain ambition mixed up in it. The layman gives up a good deal to follow Christ, but he finds himself easily offended, easily upset and easily hurt. The self is still there. It must be surrendered.

The self does not let go without a struggle. The whole of the biological urge is against it. It is an invasion of the rights of self-assertion. It is true that the demand means the possibility of self-assertion on a higher and more spiritual level, but the lower urges do not understand this and resist it. The elemental urges rise up at all talk of self-surrender and say, like Peter, 'Be it far from thee. This shall never happen unto thee.'

The step that is required to enter into the experience of what some call 'full salvation', 'entire sanctification' or 'the blessing of a clean heart' is the step of faith. Faith is an adventure in acceptance. It banks on the *bona fides* of God. It believes the character of God and what God says: 'What things soever ye desire, when we pray, believe that ye receive them, and ye shall have them' (Mk 11:24). Sanctification then awaits your acceptance. 'Blessed are those who hunger and thirst for righteousness, for they will be filled' (Mt 5:6, NIV). Someone has described faith like this: picture a small bird peering over the edge of a nest looking out in the empty air. Is it possible that the air can hold him up? Is it not plain madness to throw himself out into space? Does not death clearly await him as he goes? But some instinct stirs within him and he spreads his wings. Over the edge he goes and proves that the empty air is the element devised to hold him, and not only him but lift him up to the upper skies.

By faith, therefore, offer the self to God, and invite him to enter the depths of your being to sanctify you wholly. Throw yourself upon him, ask him to cleanse the inner springs of your being. I have stood alongside hundreds of people at the moment they invited God to purify their hearts by faith, and whenever they have made this plea in simplicity and utter sincerity, God has never failed to respond; not once. He will not let you down. Try it.

Let me say a final word about the result of inner cleansing. The peace that comes from divine forgiveness at conversion is only exceeded by that which comes from being wholly sanctified. In the language of the book of Hebrews, there remains a rest to the people of God (4:9). It is not the rest of the righteous dead that the writer is describing here for he says: 'We which have believed do enter into (this) rest.' Someone has expressed it thus: 'it is not rest from action but rest from friction.' The division in the heart is over, and strife is in the past. Such a tranquilizing trust brings a glorious feeling of joy and freedom.

We no longer need to feel defeated on the inner

battleground of the soul. Through Christ we may taste even now the joy of inward triumph, for as Henry Beecher once observed, 'A victory inside us is ten thousand times more glorious than any victory that can be outside of us.' 'God's victories,' said Dr H. Farmer, 'are won mainly on the battlefields of the human heart.' It was this victory of which Charles Wesley spoke when he wrote the immortal words:

> Come and maintain thy righteous cause,
> and let thy glorious toil succeed.
> Dispread the victory of thy Cross
> Ride on and prosper in thy deed.

It is so easy to know theoretically that merely as a matter of history, Christ has triumphed over sin, but actually to experience it in our lives is another matter. Christ is waiting not only to deliver us from the guilt and practice of sin but from those stubborn remains of self-will, self-love, and self-concern. If any are worn in the fight against sin and are looking for deliverance, then take heart for you need not look far. Christ is at hand to deliver. However it will require your consent, for God will not violate your nature. You must ask him, and as you trust and look to the cross and see yourself there hanging on that tree, you will realize then that Paul found deliverance that way, and others have found it there too. Take it from him as you look. If words fail you, then use those quoted earlier in this chapter:

> I want, dear Lord, a heart that's true and clean.
> A sunlit heart, not with a cloud between.
> A heart like thine, a heart divine, a heart as white
> as snow.
> On me, dear Lord, a heart like this bestow.

'God paints in many colours,' says Gilbert Chesterton, 'but he never paints so gorgeously as when He paints in white.'

4

A heart of praise

No other book in the Bible expresses praise more than the book of Psalms. Every furrow in this marvellous book is sown with seeds of thanksgiving. One preacher commenting on it says, 'The book of Psalms contains the whole music of the heart of man swept by the hand of his Maker.' Gratitude and gladness form the theme of many of the psalms and here, more than anywhere else in the Bible, is the exultant heart set free.

'My heart,' writes the author of Psalm 45, 'is inditing a good matter.' The margin renders the word 'inditing' as 'bubbling up'. Why is the Psalmist's heart so effervescent? Because it has 'good matter'. And what is that good matter? He is speaking about the greatness of the Creator, declaring his might amongst the people, praising the majesty of his Name, and he goes on to say, 'I speak of the things which I have made touching the king: my tongue is the pen of a ready writer.' Something interesting had happened to the Psalmist. While musing and meditating on the goodness and greatness of God, his thoughts began to bubble up within him. There was no need to sit and ponder over the subject; thoughts flowed from him like a fountain. Ideas, expressions, feelings surged through his whole being, and he found it difficult to focus them fast enough into co-ordinated thoughts. When he is finished, you have the feeling that it is because he has run out of

41

parchment, not out of praise!

In Psalm 92, the author there, it seems, is more studied in his devotions. Calmly, yet feelingly, he affirms, 'It is a good thing to give thanks unto the Lord' (verse 2). We might ask ourselves: is praise only to be given to God because it is 'a good thing'? Of course not. Praise and thankfulness, like love, are only truly satisfying when they are spontaneous, when they leap out of themselves, when they cannot be held in.

The poet Wordsworth wrote:

> My heart leaps up when I behold
> A rainbow in the sky.

This is the way it is with a heart full of praise to God. You do not have to remind yourself to be grateful. As you look up and reflect on God's goodness, your heart leaps up, too, and praise pours from you because no power on earth can stop it.

Another of the Psalmists has this to say concerning praise, 'Let every thing that hath breath praise the Lord' (Ps 150:6). Someone has wittingly said, 'You cannot say you have no breath for you need breath in order to say it.' Anyone who pauses to reflect on the wonder and goodness of God will soon discover innumerable reasons for praise. One cannot think of a more excellent thing to do with human breath than to spend it in lavish praise of the Creator.

Well might we sing with Wesley:

> Oh for a heart to praise my God,
>   A heart from sin set free,
> A heart that always feels the blood
>   So freely shed for me.

But, you might be saying, I don't *feel* like praising. The

sentiments of the Psalmist and Wesley are foreign to me.
If that is the condition of your heart, then let me share
with you how you can be set free.

First, you must understand something of how God has
constructed you as a human being. There are three main
aspects to human functioning—the will, the feelings and
the thoughts. The will has little or no power over the
feelings. It is not possible, for example, to change your
feelings by an act of will. You can't say, 'I am going to feel
different,' then try by sheer willpower to bring about a
change in your emotions. What the feelings do respond
to, however, are the thoughts. You may not be able to
change how you feel by an act of will, but you can change
how you feel through right thinking. 'Our feelings follow
our thoughts,' said a famous psychologist, 'like baby ducks
follow their mother.' This, then, is the first step on the
path of praise—think on God's goodness, fill your mind
with facts concerning his love for you, hold those thoughts
in your mind until they set fire to your emotions. It never
fails. So think now of some of the good things that surround
you. Fill your mind with them; pass them in review. One
of our hymns says:

'Count your blessings, name them one by one,
    And it will surprise you what the Lord hath done.'

It is good advice, but you will find it impossible to count all
your blessings, your arithmetic will not be good enough!
There are hundreds of things of which you are not so
much as aware. But you can think of some of them. Think
now!

Begin by thinking of the blessings of his great creation
—the fecund earth, the canopy of stars, the first flowers of
spring. Think, too, of the delightful things that come out
of the earth which grace your table day after day. I know
that it is not without some toil and struggle that things

have been drawn from the earth. However, toil alone would have been useless without the added blessing of God. Think about that!

Love and companionship are great blessings, too. Have you ever thought, for example, what your life would be like without the friendship and love of your family? If you fell sick is there not someone to smooth your pillow?

In 1930, when America was caught in the grip of economic depression, the American Association for the Advancement of Atheism raised a protest against the customary Thanksgiving Proclamation. The members of the Association said, 'The country is in a terrible state. There are hardly any jobs, there has been no rain and the fields are dry. Why should we give thanks for nothing?'

Give thanks for nothing! There was no thought given by these people to the other thousand and one blessings of life: the air they breathed and the light by which they could see. No thought for the love that burned in millions of hearts despite the setbacks and difficulties. No thought for the ripple of children's laughter or the song of the birds in the forests. How blind can men get? How low is it possible for them to fall? All around us lie a thousand things that cry out for gratitude and above them all is the fact that Christ is with us, the Brother, Helper, Saviour and Friend of all.

In many of our modern hymnals the note of hearty praise is sadly disappearing. A large number of the hymns people sing nowadays are more concerned with self than with praise to God. 'Give me a man who sings at his work,' once remarked Thomas Carlyle. Whether he himself did is not recorded but his grasp of life was certainly clear. The Christian sings best when he sings about the Lord. 'All life,' someone said, 'is set to music. It begins as a solo. Up to the age of twenty-one it is set in the minor key. Then it changes to a major. Usually afterwards comes a wedding march, and from then onwards it is a duet.

Family life changes it into an orchestra, and last of all comes the funeral march.' And what then? Well, for the Christian, his life is still set to music. John says in Revelation 7:9–10, 'After this I beheld, and, lo, a great multitude, which no man could number, of all nations, and kindreds, and people, and tongues, stood before the throne, and before the Lamb, clothed with white robes, and palms in their hands; And cried…Salvation to our God which sitteth upon the throne, and unto the Lamb.' It is true, in heaven as well as on earth, that the vision of the everlasting Christ always evokes spontaneous adoration.

However, now we must get to grips with the task of clearing our minds of morbid introspection which curbs the spirit of praise and makes life no more than self-communion. What are the things we should consider in order to have a heart full of praise?

First, give attention to the words of Psalm 100: 'Enter into his gates with thanksgiving, and into his courts with praise.' Such language, of course, points to the temple and more broadly to the place of worship. It is simply amazing how thankfulness and gratitude are nourished in the atmosphere of God's house. Those who hold that they can worship God just as well by a visit to the seaside or by communing with nature are really out of touch with the spirit of the Bible. Over and over again in the Scriptures, worship is seen at its best in God's house. That does not mean to say that worship outside of a church is unacceptable to him, but somehow the joining with fellow worshippers in the singing of God's praises gives an added joy to the worshipper and to God. 'Forsaking not the assembling of yourselves together,' is the New Testament exhortation (Heb 10:25). Even though you do not feel like going, go. There will be sweet reward awaiting you at the house of the Lord, whether that 'house' is a cottage or a cathedral.

Then you can think about the goodness of God. People

nowadays do not give much thought to God's favour towards men. Most seem to get on fairly well without him and the mood has gripped this century that God is no longer necessary to a happy existence. When Thomas Hardy wrote his poem *The Funeral of God* that, in many people's minds, meant the end of the Christian faith. A modern writer, reflecting upon this, says 'We have grown used to a Godless universe.' But this is not so with the Christian. We have not grown used to a Godless universe. Far from it! We can hardly imagine a universe in which God was not actively present. As the old Welsh proverb puts it, 'Without God, without anything.' Isaac Watts wrote:

> Thy providence is kind and large,
> Both man and beast thy bounty share.
> The whole creation is thy charge,
> But saints are thy peculiar care.

Isn't that so right? The Psalmist again says, 'Thou openest thine hand, and satisfiest the desire of every living thing' (145:16). We are more dependent upon God than we sometimes think. The great majority of us have never been desperately hungry. The fundamental cause of poverty and starvation that exists in parts of the world is not a failure of production but distribution. In some parts people starve, while in others men throw the fish back into the sea. However, this is not God's fault. His promise still operates: 'While the earth remaineth, seedtime and harvest, and cold and heat, and summer and winter, and day and night shall not cease' (Gen 8:22). For centuries God has provided and he will go on doing so. But has our sufficiency moved us to gratitude? Think about it and it should do so.

Do you enjoy good health? Then that should be a cause for great gratitude. A man visiting a military hospital which contained only the worst cases who were there for life, asked, 'Is there much coming and going here?' 'No sir,' was the answer, 'the only time we go out is when we die.' Let us be thankful when we enjoy good health.

But perhaps by far the greatest cause for gratitude in a Christian's heart is the fact of God's grace. Though his providence and care provide cause for praise, this is the crown of it all. Small wonder that when D. L. Moody, the evangelist, was meditating on this theme, the thought of its power so flashed across his soul that he dashed out into the street and shouted to the first man he met, 'Do you know grace?' The man was utterly taken aback and the only thing he could say was, 'Grace who?'

As Wesley said:

> Plenteous grace with Thee is found,
> Grace to cover all my sin.

When Paul was troubled by his thorn in the flesh, one of the things God made plain to him was the fact that whatever trial he was called to undergo God's grace would always be his comfort.

The thing that makes grace so attractive to human hearts is that it can only be offered to sinners. God may be able to love the angels, but he cannot be said to exercise grace towards them. It is only sinners who receive grace. But not only is grace offered for sin; it is offered for suffering too.

Grace is also offered for service. When the apostle Paul defends himself against those who ridiculed his work, he said, 'I laboured more abundantly than they all: yet not I, but the grace of God' (1 Cor 15:10). Paul could not have got very far in his labours for the Lord without grace, for he would have given up heart long before and turned back. God's grace, however, fortified him and nerved him ever onwards.

If you allow him, he will give you the same grace that he gave Paul and Peter and the others. Then you will truly sing:

> Grace, 'tis a charming sound
>   Harmonious to the ear.
> Heaven with its echoes shall resound,
>   And all the earth shall hear.
>   Grace!

5

A heart at peace with God

Sooner or later in this world every man and woman comes
to a time when life seems plunged into shadow. At such
times the heart becomes anxious and full of unrest. Even
the strongest sometimes break under the strain. It is said
of J. Pierpoint Morgan, the American financier, that when
his wife died he was so distraught and downcast that for
days he cried like a child. And Morgan was considered
one of the hardest men of his time.

In an hour when shadows are breaking in upon the soul,
is there anything God can do to keep the heart at peace?
We know he can cleanse and make it new, but can he keep
it buoyant and sustain it above the waves of adversity that
fling themselves against the Christian's life?

He can!

The apostle Paul in Philippians 4:7 says, 'And the
peace of God, which passeth all understanding, shall keep
your hearts and minds through Christ Jesus.' What a
promise this is! The word *keep* in the original means
'sentinel' and was used to denote the keeper of a castle—
someone responsible for watching the gate of a fort,
admitting only those whose right it was to enter. When the
invading armies were approaching, it was the sentinel's
duty to give the alert and warn the garrison of danger.
This is precisely the function that God's peace performs in
the soul. It warns the heart of approaching trouble and

49

guards against the entry of any intruder into the deep, inner sanctuary of the heart.

No one can keep trouble out of his life. Christians are open to its onslaught as much as anyone else. Some sincere Christians believe that in this world it is the good people who have a bad time, and the bad people who seem to get off scot free. They quote the names of those bad ones who seem to secure everything their grasping hands reach out for, and then place it by the list of those good people who never seem to get anywhere. If the problem is examined fairly, one will discover that, generally speaking, troubles come to us all, and as the King says in Hamlet:

> They come not in single spies,
> But in battalions.

We all have our fair share of trouble, and when it does come, it seems to come all at once. Sickness strikes, perhaps bringing with it financial worry. As if this is not enough, business difficulties increase and the harmony of the home is disturbed. The world suddenly turns grey and life doesn't seem worth living. In such circumstances, how is it possible for one's heart to remain at peace? One answer is to remove the difficulties. If circumstances alter then peace will return. Peace, however, is not something produced by circumstances; it is a state of being. Circumstances cannot make it or affect it when once it is there, for the peace of God is independent. It bows down to no one.

In the depths of the human heart, it is possible to enjoy a peace which God alone can produce. Despite the troubles that afflict life, in the depth of the heart of a Christian all can be tranquil and serene. This great truth is admirably expressed by Harriet Beecher Stowe:

> When winds are raging o'er the upper ocean,
> And billows wild content with angry roar,

'Tis said, far down beneath the wild commotion
That peaceful stillness reigneth evermore.
So too the heart that knows thy love, O Purest,
There is a temple sacred evermore,
And all the babble of life's angry voices,
Dies in hushed silence at its peaceful door.
Far, far away the roar of passion dieth,
And loving thoughts rise calm and peacefully
And no rude storm, how fierce so e'er it flieth,
Disturbs the soul that dwells, O Lord, in Thee.

There are some things in life that come without working
or striving. Growth is one of them. 'Who of you,' said
Jesus, 'by worrying can add a single hour to his life?'
(Mt 6:27, NIV). It is impossible to grow by toiling at it.
Growth is the result of a natural process that comes without
anxious effort. So it is with peace. 'The fruit of the Spirit,'
said the apostle Paul, when writing to the Galatians, 'is
love, joy, peace. . . .' One preacher has pointed out that
you cannot make peace any more than you can make love.
Both are products of the soul and cannot be made; they
just come. A person grows by simply absorbing the provi-
sion of his environment and living life in an ordinary and
natural way. Just so with the Christian. As the life of the
believer is lived in close co-operation with the Lord,
peace flows into the heart just as surely as blood flows into
the veins. And as we have said, circumstances make little
difference to it either.

Augustine once went into the desert to seek peace and
found it everywhere but in his own heart. When at last he
did find it, he was in the heart of busy Milan. Christians
who enjoy the peace of God in their lives are not troubled
by circumstances. Though trouble knocks at their door,
their inner resources are always equal to the need. In the
midst of this 'eternal whirl and fiddle', as John Stuart
Black called this life, nothing can disturb that central
calm. The keeper of the castle, God's wonderful peace,

guards their soul, and though it does not keep troubles away, it stoutly resists their entrance into the inner region of the heart. They can come so far but no further. They can affect the body, but not the soul. There deep tranquillity reigns.

There are three great enemies which threaten to filch the Christian's peace, and they stand continually before every heart, waiting for an unguarded moment when they can invade. If, however, God's peace is on guard, then nothing can enter and nothing disturb. Let us look at each of these in turn.

The first enemy of peace is fear

In some ways, of course, fear is a good thing. It keeps some on the straight and narrow. Fear of being found out sometimes keeps the young man from being tempted to commit a crime. Fear of being run over enables us to negotiate our way through the traffic-infested streets without mishap.

However, in other ways fear is a bad thing. There is, for example, the fear of want. Millions have faced this fear from the beginning of history—and millions still face it. Then there is the fear of sickness. How often do we pick up a newspaper and see the name of someone we know well who has been struck down by some paralysing sickness, and the thought shapes itself: 'It could have been me.' Or take the fear of death. Despite all the gospel says of the promise of life after death, there are still some Christians who are afraid to die. It seems that the exit from life is surrounded by so many shadows that cause thousands to shrink back in dread.

These are not the only fears that creep up to the door of the human heart. The psychologists tell us that when a child is born it has two fears: the fear of falling and the fear of loud noises, but before it is twenty-one years old it has gathered a thousand other fears into its mind.

God's way of meeting fear in the heart is by spreading his love through every part. The Bible says. 'Perfect love casteth out fear' (1 Jn 4:18). The reason why so many earthly fears are quelled in our early days is because, in simple trust, we learn to rely much upon the love of those who care for us. As children we knew that whenever we fell, or were hurt in any way, loving hands were there to care for us and to soothe the pain out of our hurts. Such love took away our fear, and so it is with divine love. If trust of an earthly parent can take away all fear, then how much more that of a loving, heavenly Father? God's love drives all dread away, and we know that he will never permit anything to happen to us that does not first pass his permissive test. With love in our hearts, all dread is driven away.

Another enemy of peace is self-pity

Self-pity is more subtle in its approach to the soul than any other enemy of peace. It advances towards the human heart in the guise of a friend, and, once admitted, produces the downfall from within. This is the way it works. It brings its grievance before the keeper of the gate and argues out its points with eloquence. 'Why should all this happen to me?' is one of its popular cries. 'I can't stand any more, and unless something is done right away then I may as well lie down and die.' Perhaps we are all aware of the tenor of self-pity's tone. However, if peace is to prevail in the human heart then self-pity must not be let in through the gate.

It is, in actual fact, an evil thing. It turns molehills into mountains. It misconstrues the best intentions. It exaggerates trivialities and gives them tremendous dimensions. Little inconveniences become burdens, and soon the whole of life is coloured by it. In such a mood one whines through life ever ready to pour a list of troubles into the ear of anyone who is unfortunate enough to stop and listen.

If such a state is encouraged, disorder reigns in the heart. However, God's peace is well aware of self-pity's subtlety and will not allow it past the gate. It bids it keep back, for in the heart that is garrisoned by God's love the only pity that is permitted is that which flows out to others. It seems to be a law of the spiritual life that we keep only that which we give away. When love is allowed to flow out to others, the life develops on a healthy and sound basis, but once it is turned inwards then it becomes sour and serves no purpose.

This is the way in which God saves us from the distress into which self-pity can lure us. He shows us that around us there are thousands 'who are dying for a little bit of love.' The world is desperately in need of pity and care and concern. Is it just to expend upon ourselves the love that others so greatly need? This stabbing question will bring us to our senses if we are in danger of lapsing into this mood, and when we are tempted, then let us turn our eyes on to the one who had more reason for self-pity than anyone—Jesus Christ, the Son of God. He was betrayed by one of his party, denied by another of the same band, spat upon, scourged, beaten and finally crucified. However, not once did he show any concern for himself. Love in him flowed out to others, and when they tore his bleeding body with the nails, it only caused the blood to flow by which all men could be forgiven. In such a heart peace ruled and reigned. It can rule, too, in yours if your thoughts are on the Saviour and not on yourself.

A third enemy of peace is irritation

Have you ever been irritated? If you have then you know how it can soon lure you almost into a state of panic.

Perhaps someone has said something about your work, or even your person, and you feel the irritation working up in your soul. It might not be serious enough to cause an outburst of anger, but only enough to cause a deep feeling of irritability. There are other ways it can come, too: a train missed, a letter mislaid, a 'phone call forgotten, and soon our hearts are filched of peace. We find ourselves saying things we are sorry for afterwards. One of the interesting things about the life of Jesus Christ when he was on this earth was this—he never hurried, never worried and was never flurried. Trace his life through the gospels and you will not find one instance where he was ever late for an appointment, nor is it even recorded that he made a wrong decision. It seems his life was poised and completely free from the irritations that continually cause us annoyance.

'Ah,' but you say, 'if he had lived today in our speed-orientated society, he would have found it more difficult to control his affairs. There is much more today to cause annoyance and irritation than in the days when Christ was alive.' I wonder!

What could be more irritating than Peter's obvious impetuosity? What greater reason for annoyance than to be awakened from sleep while upon the lake, because of the fear that had gripped the disciples? How easily he could have been irritated by the senseless questions of the Pharisees. Never once did he show annoyance over the problems and difficulties of life. In all the days of his life on earth, he appears poised in the plan and purpose of God, and from him there comes an atmosphere of deep tranquillity and peace.

The reason for Christ's inner harmony is easy to understand. He walked every step in the Father's will. Each day he sought the Almighty's directions, and never went anywhere unless first of all conscious that God was with him. He was always at the place his Father wanted him to be,

and, because of this, he never had any regrets to disturb
the deep tranquillity of his soul.

When life is lived in harmony with God's will then
irritation's annoying power can never reach the calm
depths of the heart at peace with God.

6

A solid heart—fixed on God

One of the things the Psalmist has to say about the heart
that trusts in God is that it is 'established'. You cannot
help but like the word. It is used everywhere in the Psalms
as relating to the foundation of the world. In Psalm 112:8
the Psalmist writes, 'His heart is established.' In the pre-
ceding verse, he says that the godly heart is 'fixed'. One is
reminded of the hymn:

> My heart is fixed, Eternal God,
>   Fixed on Thee, fixed on Thee.
> And my immortal choice is made,
>   Christ for me!

There is something stable and solid about a heart that
trusts in God. The same strength and steadfastness are
found in it as are seen in the material universe. It stands
like some towering cliff of granite, rising out of the heaving
sea, firm, solid and immovable. In the flux and flow of life
the Christian's heart remains 'fixed'. Not 'in a fix', as one
preacher pointed out when commenting on this verse in
the Psalms, but held by the Almighty in such a grip that
nothing, absolutely nothing, can loosen it from its mooring
in God.

We might well raise the enquiry in connection with the
established heart as to what extent it is fixed. Now and

again one sees a shop with the prominent sign 'Established 1850'. Upon examination, one discovers that in over a hundred years the shop has never grown in size or custom, and the only thing that has happened in a hundred years is that the business is a century older. To be established does not mean to be stuck in a rut. Another Psalm appears to shed a ray of light on this point. 'He brought me up...out of an horrible pit, out of the miry clay, and set my feet upon a rock, and established my goings' (40:2). 'Established my goings'!—doesn't that sound strange? How can one be established and set going? What does it mean?

Well, if it means anything, it is an indication of what takes place in a man who is fixed in God. He is not only steady in his anchorage in God, but that same steadiness characterizes his whole walk. Because his heart is fixed, his feet do not slide, and as he walks through life it is with purposeful aim and resolute determination. In this way his goings as well as his heart are established.

The Christian stands in a world beset with all kinds of enticements. On every hand the temptations of life beat down upon him. A thousand and one things harass him, continually threatening to break the ties that hold him to the Lord. One of the reasons why a Christian does not succumb to the temptation of the world around him is because he has no doubts about the ability of God to hold him. Let us be clear on this. No Christian can hope to remain solid and immovable in a world of change if he has doubt in his heart. There are some things about which you may doubt in life without it having much effect upon you. You can doubt, for instance, about whether the dew comes up from the earth or whether it comes down, and it will not have much effect upon your life. However, you simply cannot afford to have any doubts about the sufficiency of God, his eternal salvation and his keeping power. If Christians are overbalanced and their hearts are overturned, then it is usually because doubt first steals into their hearts. It undermines the life and soon grows from doubt to denial.

For the Christian heart to be fixed, it means that there are certain facts about God which are held to and believed with confidence. Let me use an illustration. A pilot who is responsible for bringing a ship into harbour depends mainly upon the existence of certain fixed points about which he is absolutely certain. He knows they never move and whether it be a lighthouse, a rock or a headland, he depends, to a great extent, upon their solidarity. If a lighthouse slipped or a headland moved, he could well plunge his passengers into disaster. However, everyone knows that a lighthouse does not slide; it is fixed. Navigators do not take their bearings from the clouds they take them from the stars.

So it is with the Christian. As he moves through life, he makes his progress by constant reference to definite points. He must not only know what he believes, he must believe it with the full assurance of understanding. He must know, as Wesley knew, the experience of being anchored to the Rock:

> Fixed on this ground will I remain
>   Though my heart fail and flesh decay,
> This anchor shall my soul sustain
>   When earth's foundations melt away.
> Mercy's full power I then shall prove,
>   Loved with an everlasting love.

This question of assurance and confidence in God's ability to keep is more essential in Christian experience than perhaps many realize. D. L. Moody said that the man who has his feet fixed on the Rock of Salvation can say with certainty, 'I know'. There is no doubt about that. Confidence in God's power creates a deep sense of assurance in the depth of the heart. Those who lack assurance in this respect plod their way wearily through the Christian life when all the time God waits to give them the deep understanding that all things have been completed by Christ, and that trust appropriates all God's gifts and blessings to the heart.

Some doubt their salvation. John Wesley didn't. On 24th May 1738, in that little room in Aldersgate Street, he says, 'There was given to me an assurance that He had taken away my sins, even mine, and saved me from the law of sin and death.' Some Christian denominations teach: 'It is not possible for a person to know with any certainty that he is the recipient of the grace of God.' There are many church members who cannot say with any degree of certainty that Christ is theirs. They are always hoping, and thus their testimony is often negative.

When we step into the Bible, however, we come into the full blaze of the sunlight of God's keeping power and he shows us, without any shadow of doubt, that when a person comes to Christ then all God's power is bent on keeping that saint in the narrow way.

With God's power working for us, why should we ever entertain the slightest of doubts. With our feet on the Rock and our hand in his, then we should never fear, for as the hymnist said:

> He will keep me till the river
>   Rolls its waters at my feet,
> Then He'll bear me safely over,
>   Where the loved ones I shall meet.

Yes, it is true. Assurance of heart can be achieved by any Christian, and in the knowledge of that experience, the soul feels safe and secure.

There are two things, however, that the believer who knows the experience of the established heart must continually realize. It is maintained by faith and hope.

The writer to the Hebrews uses a beautiful expression: 'Having an high priest over the house of God; let us draw near with a true heart in full assurance of faith' (10:21–22). This, then, is the language of Christian certainty. It is the strong tones of the established heart. There is no room for half-assurance here, for where faith is in action, it takes all that God has to give. When you remember that God has promised in his word to *keep* his children, then there is no reason in the world why any Christian should doubt. Peter says that all those who are God's children are 'kept by the power of God' (1 Pet 1:5). Think of it! The same power that pulses in the ocean tides and that guides the sun and stars and systems works on behalf of the Christian to guide his life and keep him safe in a world of sin. God's power is the Christian's tower of strength. It encompasses him, defends him, sustains him, secures him. Though all the devils in hell hurl themselves at him, bent on obtaining his downfall, there is nothing their attacks can achieve, providing he is standing firm in faith. He can say with the Psalmist: 'As the mountains are round about Jerusalem, so the Lord is round about his people' (125:2).

However, it must be remembered that all this is dependent upon faith. That is why the writer to the Hebrews encourages us to draw near in full assurance. There is no need for anyone to depend upon feelings when faith is available. Faith is simply taking God at his word. In the words of the simple acrostic, it is:

Forsaking
All
I
Trust
Him

Never forget that there is solid ground for a full assurance and it is based in the eternal God.

The second thing that is necessary to the maintenance of the Christian's establishment is hope. The writer to the Hebrews talks about the 'full assurance of hope'. He then goes on to describe in beautiful language: 'Which hope we have as an anchor of the soul, both sure and stedfast, and which entereth into that within the veil; Whither the forerunner is for us entered, even Jesus...' (6:19–20).

Philip Mauro points out in relation to this text that it is difficult for us to appreciate fully the beauty and aptness of these words. Living as we do in times far removed from the early days of the New Testament, it is easy to misunderstand what sort of anchor the writer is referring to here. We are used to seeing the great iron affair with two flukes carried at the bow of our modern ships. The purpose of such an anchor is to hold the ship firm in bad weather, or when it is required that the ship remains stable. However, the anchor that the writer to the Hebrews is referring to is not an anchor that holds us fast to the bottom of the sea, but an anchor that draws us near to God. 'The figure,' says Mauro, 'is taken from the practice that prevailed in old times in the harbours of the Mediterranean and other inland seas. In every harbour, as may be seen to this day, was a great stone immovably embedded in the ground near the water's edge. That rock, as we understand, was the anchoria (Greek *agkura*). It served ordinarily as a mooring for the little vessels of those days; but it also had another function. Sometimes a little ship could not by means of its sail make its way to a secure mooring within the harbour. In such cases a 'forerunner' would go ashore in a small boat with a line which would be made fast to the anchoria. That was sure and steadfast, being of ample strength and immovably embedded in the ground. Therefore, those on the ship had only to hold fast the line and by means of it and by patient, persistent effort, gradually draw near to the shore.'

What a picture of Christian hope!

According to the poet, 'Hope springs eternal in the human breast,' but the unfortunate thing is that many people have no real grounds or basis upon which to hope. The real beauty of the Christian hope is that it has a solid ground upon which to rest. It is fixed upon the fact that Christ, the forerunner, has entered into the heavenly home and has established there a line between himself and us. That is why we can stand up bravely to the shocks and assaults of temptation. We are sure that there is a line between us and the Lord, and that by our faith and hope in him, we can, if patient, one day meet him in that land beyond the grave.

It is important to notice, too, that the Christian's deep security does not take the form of immunity to trials and tribulation. It lies rather in the triumph over these and all the other hazards that beset the path of the traveller in Christ. Though God permits trials to come and, in the necessary discipline of life, allows many sorrows to over-take us, yet he desires to teach us, as Dr Paul S. Rees suggests, 'that our confidence in His grip is sometimes more necessary than our consciousness of it.'

The established heart begins the day a man is converted. Its feeling of deep assurance proceeds each day that he walks in touch with the Lord. One day when Christ returns, it will be finally and fully consummated in that deep, eternal assurance that there will be no parting or broken fellowship in the eternal age. However, the fact that Christ has not yet come does not affect the established heart. He knows that same security now that he will enjoy in eternity. Only the circumstances will be changed.

7

*A prayerful heart—
in tune with heaven*

The Psalmist, in his matchless soliloquy in Psalm 27 says, 'When thou saidst, Seek ye my face; my heart said unto thee, thy face, Lord, will I seek' (v. 8). There were no difficulties concerning prayer in the life of the writer of this psalm. When the invitation came from on high, it found a ready response in his heart. The difficulties people talk about in connection with prayer had no place in the Psalmist's life. He needed no second invitation to pray; it was his delight—not a burden but a blessing.

Many Christians, who are otherwise deeply spiritual, confess that their greatest difficulties are in the realm of prayer. Some who find it easy to witness, preach, sing, work, write, visit, or any of the other avenues of service will tell you that they find it hard to pray. This probably is more real than we first imagine, for unless God finds a ready response in our hearts to pray, then we cannot claim to be on the closest terms with him, for prayer is nothing more than conversation with God.

There was something about the prayer life of Jesus Christ that one day caused the disciples to ask, 'Lord, teach us to pray.' Nowhere is it recorded that they ever asked Christ to teach them to preach. They were nourished by the uplifting prayers of Jeremiah and Isaiah (for they were regularly chanted in the temple), but still, when they heard Jesus talk with God, they wanted him to teach them to pray. We may well also make that request now: 'Lord, teach us to pray.'

Some people, on the other hand, love prayer. They are all too few, of course, but in the Christian church there have been those in every decade who delighted to be prodigal with the hours they spent before the throne of grace. Wesley rose every morning at four to pray. Praying Hyde was astir at five. If we are honest with ourselves, however, we will confess that prayer is more often a duty than a delight. We fall upon our knees and are almost glad when the exercise is over; then we move out to salve our conscience in some active work. But this is where we make a tragic mistake. We cannot really get on with God until we know how to converse with him properly.

There are some Christians who would tell you that they could not get their work done each day unless they spent one, two or even three full hours in prayer. And there are others who would confess that five minutes upon their knees is all they can afford. We are a long way from the spirit of the Psalmist here. Such people who spend only minutes in prayer find it difficult to understand how the others can pray for hours. It seems a mystery to them that prayer is counted in hours and not in seconds.

Some too, feel a deep sense of unworthiness because they do not share the Psalmist's response when the time for prayer comes around in the day. They say that when they pray they do not always 'feel like it', and because of this they feel a sense of guilt. All this arises from misunderstandings concerning prayer, and it is with these that we concern ourselves here.

In order to think this through clearly, let us put our observations into these propositions.

Prayer is reality

There are many sincere Christians who feel that prayer is

merely an exercise in auto-suggestion. They admit the psychological values but that is as far as they go. However, if prayer was simply auto-suggestion, then we would, in fact, be giving ourselves to unreality. Someone has put it thus:

To talk with God no breath is lost—talk on!
To walk with God no strength is lost—walk on!
To wait on God no time is lost—wait on!

Prayer is reality. When we pray something happens. A Christian once confessed in a midweek prayer service, 'I have let down my prayer life and that is why I have been defeated every day.' Defeat in prayer means defeat in practice. Dr E. Stanley Jones says, 'If you don't have a quiet time in the morning, you will probably have an unquiet time at night.'

During the American Constitutional Convention, when delegates gathered to write the words and frame the Constitution, they had been there for four weeks without writing a word when Benjamin Franklin rose to his feet and addressed the group thus, 'I have lived a long time and the longer I live the more convincing proofs I see that God governs in the affairs of men. I, therefore, beg leave to move that henceforth prayers imploring the assistance of heaven and its blessing upon our deliberations be held in this assembly every morning.' The motion was carried, and from that moment they made rapid progress and produced the Constitution which Gladstone said, 'was the most remarkable work to have been produced by the human intellect at a single stroke.' Prayer brought reality.

Prayer is renewal

Modern life is lived under so many pressures that, like a battery, it soon runs down. That is why Christians so often need to be recharged. Prayer is the way. When we reach out to God in prayer we touch the infinite resources of heaven. Jesus knew the value of this, for often at the end of some special mission or miracle, he would turn away from the crowds and get alone with God to pray. Whenever he came from those periods of prayer he was charged with divine energy, and in this way he was able to maintain that deep spiritual power that characterized his ministry.

It must not be mistaken for a 'shot in the arm' experience that lifts us up for a while and then lets us down again, as would a drug or some special vitamins. It is not a mere stimulant, but a complete renewal. As we spend time with the Lord in prayer and adoration of him, he puts within us a new transfusion of his power. The abundant life of which Jesus speaks comes in when prayer is made. It is the opening of the soul to God, and as we spend this time conversing with the Lord, vitality and virtue flow from him to us.

There was a certain occasion in the life of Christ when the crowds sought him and he could not be found. He was spending time in prayer, and to him that was more important than standing before the multitudes. Without prayer, then, his whole ministry would have suffered, and it was necessary for him to be renewed in order that the life of God might flow out to others. Much of our lives are spent amongst the things that are relatively unimportant. We are busy over nothing. When we get alone with the Lord then the whole of life takes on its real meaning. Things are placed in their proper order and we see life as a whole again.

An artist who loved to paint outdoor scenes used to keep at his side a collection of beautifully-coloured stones. When asked the reason for this, he replied, 'I have to wash out my eyes continually in the colours of nature.' In other words, he would renew his vision by a glimpse of the colours, and this is what we do when we pray. Our spiritual

eyesight becomes dimmed by constant use, and then we
take a look at Christ. In his light we see things as they
really are. We wash ourselves in his colour, and we go
back to life renewed, refreshed and re-invigorated. Prayer
washes us, cleanses us, refreshes us, and sends us back to
our tasks renewed.

Prayer is release

There are so many aspects of prayer that it is difficult to
think of them all in one chapter. There is, for example,
request—when we ask God for things. There is, too,
adoration—when we worship God for who and what he
is. Then there is confession—the pursuit of holiness, or
intercession—the art of moving God through prayer. Then
there is thanksgiving—the gratitude of heart that does not
forget to thank, and there is consecration—the fresh
surrender of the heart to God. There are so many aspects
of prayer that clamour for attention but space will only
permit this one further aspect—that prayer is release.

Release from what? Well, first of all, it is release from
ourselves!

So much of life is self-centred, but when we kneel to
pray we automatically confess that, by that very action,
we are turning from ourselves to another. Someone had
said that the 'greatest difficulty in the Christian life is to
cross out the *I*', and if anyone disagrees with that it can
only be because they have never tried it. The crossing out
of the personal pronoun is, indeed, a problem. But prayer
can do it! It takes our mind from self and sets it upon the
living God.

Prayer is release from our burdens, too

A Christian businessman says that when he prays his desk
is cleared far more easily than when he does not. The

reason for that, of course, is simple. When he prays, his mind is taken up by thoughts of God and, because of this, he is lifted above his problems. In that realm he looks down upon his life, not around. Everyone knows that an eagle is never disturbed by the muddy pool upon the ground because he possesses the ability to fly over it. In prayer, the heart draws near to God and sees things as he sees them. Problems and burdens take their proportions from him, and it is surprising how small a problem becomes when placed against the wisdom and power and majesty of God.

Finally, prayer releases us from the grip of doubt.

One of the most distracting things in the Christian life is the occurrence of doubt that over and over again seeps into the mind at the most unusual times. Part of the devil's work seems to be the sowing of doubts in the mind, and there is hardly a period of any day when, somewhere, he is not at work. However, prayer is an explosive force and a moment spent in communion with God can blast every doubt the devil can bring.

Those experienced in prayer tell us that to fight the doubts is to encourage them. They must be outwitted by lifting them before the throne of God to let God show them up for what they are. There are times when the devil causes us to doubt our own salvation. One look at the cross can remedy this. As you look at Calvary and ask yourself why Christ hung there, the answer soon comes, 'Behold the Lamb of God, which taketh away the sin of the world' (Jn 1:29). Perhaps you doubt God's interest in your life. How many times does the devil delight in taunting Christians about God's care? 'God has forgotten you,' he seems to say, 'and he has no further interest in your life.' In such a moment, bring it before God in prayer. Think on his word. Has he not promised to engrave your name upon the palm of his hand? How can God ever forget when your name is written there?

Then there is the very real doubt the devil brings about whether God is really there or not. He will often slip up to your side when you kneel, and say, 'You fool, you are simply talking into thin air.' How can we beat him then? Well, the thing to do is to pray on; but to prayer you should add imagination. A lot has been said and written about the place of imagination in prayer, and what I say now cannot be too strongly emphasized.

Imagination is a gift of God. Use it properly and it will open heaven further to you. There is no doubt that when the disciples prayed in the Upper Room at Pentecost, they prayed to God and his Son upon the throne. They had never seen God but they had seen his Son, and they could well imagine him seated at the Father's right hand. For them prayer was brought into focus in the person of Christ. It can be for you, too. You may never have seen Jesus, but you can attempt to imagine him there at your side. If you sanctify your imagination, it is simply amazing what a new sphere it can bring you into. If turn from your New Testament, where so often you see the Christ of Galilee, and picture him there with you in your room, there would be no further difficulties with doubts, fears or anxious thoughts. You would have no trouble either in what to say and how to say it. Prayer would flow from you. The Psalmist said: 'I have set the Lord always before me' (16:8). In imagination, you can shut your eyes on earth and open them in heaven. See God, and prayer will flow from you as water flowed from the rock.

As God calls, you will hasten to answer. 'When thou saidst, Seek ye my face; my heart said unto thee, Thy face, Lord, will I seek' (Ps 27:8).

8

A tender heart and true

In his letter to the Ephesians, chapter 4, verse 32, the apostle Paul encourages the Christians in Ephesus to be ready to forgive and swift to pardon. He uses a beautiful expression to describe the condition of heart every Christian should develop, and he tells them that above all things they should be without anger, and kind and tenderhearted.

In a world where, at some time or other, everyone receives a hard knock, it is difficult to understand how the heart can be kept from becoming unforgiving and unsympathetic. Without the help of Christ, of course, it is well-nigh impossible, but given his strength and grace, it is simply amazing what God can achieve in the human heart to make it tender and forgiving.

It is, in fact, possible for every Christian's heart to become like God's in this respect. This was the cry of the hymn-writer when he wrote:

> Come, let us sing of a wonderful love,
>   Tender and true,
> Out of the heart of the Father above,
>   Streaming to me and to you.
> Wonderful Love
>   Dwells in the heart of the Father above.

71

Not only does it dwell in the heart of the Father above—it can dwell in ours, too!

The word 'tenderhearted' which appears in Ephesians 4:32 has to do, I believe, with the issue of forgiveness. The context describes how Christians, when faced by circumstances that provoke them to anger, should choose not to become angry, but instead develop a heart that is full of compassion and love. To reinforce his argument the apostle appeals to the Ephesian converts to forgive those who had hurt them, 'even as God for Christ's sake hath forgiven you.'

Psychologists tell us that forgiveness is healthy. 'When we nurse grievances,' they say, 'we poison our minds and nurture ill-health at the very heart of our being.' If anger is allowed to burn in our hearts, it will become a fire that eats its way through our whole personality. Those who have forgiven great injustices tell us that the burden that rolls from the mind is almost as great as that which is removed when they were first forgiven by Christ.

True Christians do it almost every day, and what a blessing it brings. When Dr Barnardo was just a medical student in London, he was involved in a drunken brawl while doing some evangelistic work in a tavern. He was there to sell Bibles and got mixed up in a fight. When the ruffians who had set upon him had finished, he was left with a bruised and bleeding body. Two of his ribs were crushed, and it was six weeks before he could move again. When the police urged him to press charges against those who had harmed him, Barnardo refused. 'I have begun with the gospel,' he said, 'and I am determined not to end with the law.'

In April 1923 Molly Ellis was snatched by murderous hands into the hills of Kohat. Those responsible for law and order in that part of the world planned an attack in order to rescue her from what might be her death. However, a little Englishwoman made her way into the hills before they had time to march, and rescued Molly. Her name was Mrs Starr. She was a nurse and had been married to a missionary doctor who had been killed by those same treacherous hands. Though her husband had been brutally murdered, she refused to return home and stood at the post, nursing the sick and caring for those who needed her medical attentions. The Afridis were nonplussed by such a demonstration of forgiveness, and when she made her way into the hills to rescue Molly Ellis, they could not resist her. Her forgiveness had so melted the hearts of these people that when she walked among them they had no heart to refuse her the life she asked for.

When we look into the lives of the famous in history, we discover that, over and over again, many whose names shine as the stars are those who, having been hurt, found it possible to forgive. I think of Milton, singing so beautifully in his *Paradise Lost*, then of Bunyan, imprisoned in body though not in spirit. These, and many others, testify to the fact that it is not so much what overtakes us that matters, but what our reaction is to it. Bunyan did not bear a grudge but turned his interests to higher things. Paul, the apostle, when beaten and stoned, did not retire from the fight to nurse his wounds and lament his fortune but pressed on with a heart full of forgiveness.

Where there is no resentment there can be no hate. Narvez, the Spanish patriot, when dying, was asked by his father if he had forgiven his enemies. Narvez turned to his father and said, 'I have no enemies. I have shot them all.' That certainly is one way of getting rid of them, but forgiveness is better. Scientists agree that before a pearl can be made the little oyster in the shell, deep down in the ocean, must be the victim of a hurt. This is what takes place. A tiny irritant, such as a grain of sand, or some other alien substance, enters the oyster's shell, and immediately all the resources of the little sea creature rush to the rescue. To save any further hurt or damage, the oyster exudes a secretion which eventually hardens and forms a pearl. If nature had not endowed it with the ability to correct the harm a grain of sand could cause, then its life would be in danger. However, nature provides it with a solution which not only heals the wound but produces a pearl!

Almost every day of our lives we have to face tiny irritants that can so easily cause annoyance. Perhaps we are the subject of a piece of gossip or the victim of some cruel injustice. Immediately we feel the wound burning and throbbing within our hearts. At such a time the Christian has a power he can call upon that is reserved especially by God for healing wounds that life has made. It is called *grace*!

There is no life in which trouble and disappointment do not play a part, and at such times God is ever ready with his grace. Those who love him deeply know how to draw upon it in times of trial. Paul knew how to do it when he set out to evangelize the heathen with a stake in his flesh. He was able to staunch the bleeding of his heart by forgiving those who blocked his path, and by meeting enmity with clemency.

One of the strangest things in life is the various reactions that trouble produces in people's lives. The same hurt that cripples one person sweetens another. One ugly rumour can cause a person to become disgruntled and sour, but the same thing happening to another can be turned by them from a stumbling-block into a stepping-stone. We all shrink from the disappointments that life brings, but if we really thought about it, many of those things have a ministry to perform. They are, in fact, golden opportunities for us to make something else witness to the transforming power of the grace of God.

Many a Christian's life has been almost destroyed by his nursing the desire for revenge. It is deep-rooted within all of us, and the desire to get even is something we all feel in moments when we are the victim of some injury. Hatred and revenge, if left in the heart and not dealt with immediately, only cause the wound to fester and become gangrenous. However just the resentment may be, there is simply no argument for allowing it to remain in the soul. It is a deadly poison and the only thing it can do to the heart is destroy it.

No person in the history of the world had greater cause for bearing malice than Jesus. Though he had many bitter enemies, he had no enmity. By forgiveness he had destroyed it. That is why the cross of Christ towers over the centuries and proudly displays the message of Christ's forgiveness when empires that were founded on hate have crumbled into the dust and vanished. The cross holds out its wide arms to all who cling to hate. Paul reminds us that when we look at Calvary and see how God forgave us for that, there is simply no argument left to us to hold on to hate. He seems to say that if God has forgiven you for the cross, then who are you to hold resentment in such circumstances?

It is true, of course, that there is a legitimate anger that can be used to serve the purpose of life. It is said in the New Testament that Jesus looked on them 'with anger, being grieved for the hardness of their hearts' (Mk 3:5). Here anger was grief, and if anger becomes grief at what is happening to others, then it is the way of Christ. If it is just personal resentment against what is happening to you then it is wrong and unchristian.

Why is it that in history peace treaties have only lasted on an average for two-and-a-half years? For one simple reason: they were founded on revenge. An American general, speaking before an audience at the end of the 1939–45 War, said, 'Now that the war is over we must hate, hate and hate.' Vigorous applause greeted the statement. However, as Einsworth Resiner has said, 'The dice are loaded against enmities. The natural affinity of human nature is goodwill.' When someone remonstrated with Lincoln that he had forgiven an enemy, he replied, 'Our business is to get rid of our enemies, isn't it? Well, I have got rid of this one by turning him into a friend.'

What a wonderful front the church of Christ would present to the world if, instead of bitterness and resentment, she was to show love.

When Tokichi Ishii, awaiting his death sentence, stumbled accidentally upon the passage in the New Testament, 'Father, forgive them,' he said that in a flash he saw the whole meaning of Christianity. 'That verse,' he said, 'pierced my heart like a five-inch nail,' and he was forever changed.

It is because God forgives us that we can forgive others. If we shut others off from our forgiveness, then we shut ourselves off from God's forgiveness. We should never forget that no one has ever treated us worse than we have treated God. God doesn't ask us to do something he himself will not do. Our hearts, therefore, are to be tender—ready to forgive. We must forgive—we can do no other in the light of Calvary love.

If we do not bear a heart that is tender and forgiving, then the same thing will happen to us that happened to the man in the story Jesus once told. That man was once forgiven a debt of three million pounds, but he refused to forgive a man who owed him twenty pounds. He handed his debtor over to the torturers until he paid up all his debts. If God was to hand us over to the torturers—enmity, hatred, conflict, unrest—what would happen to us?

> God's way is the best!
> It is the way of forgiveness—
> It is the way the Master went;
> Should not the servant tread it still?

9

A burning heart

One of the most memorable meetings recorded in the New Testament is that of Jesus and the two disconsolate travellers on the road to Emmaus. The story is depicted for us in chapter 24 of Luke's gospel. Picture the scene with me. Cleopas and his companion (some think his wife) are returning from Jerusalem to their home in Emmaus following the death of their Master a few days before. Their spirits are, indeed, low. Dejected and disillusioned, they move slowly along the road towards home, sharing together their perplexity and despair.

Suddenly, up from behind, comes a stranger, walking faster, who falls into step beside them. Naturally they stop discussing their private grief and continue their journey in silence. 'You seemed to be in deep discussion about something,' says the stranger. 'What are you so concerned about?' Cleopas replies, 'You must be the only person in all Jerusalem who hasn't heard about the terrible things that happened there last week.' 'What things?' asks the stranger. Cleopas then begins to outline the sad story. 'It's now the third day since it happened. Jesus of Nazareth, a great prophet and a mighty teacher, was crucified on a Roman cross in Jerusalem. We thought, because of his miracles, that he was the predicted Messiah, but it cannot be so. And, to make matters worse, some women from our group reported to us that after visiting his tomb, they saw an angel who told them that Jesus was alive. When several of our men went to investigate, it was true that his body was not there. Now we don't know what to believe.'

It is precisely at this point that the stranger, none other than the risen Lord himself, begins to expound the Scriptures to them. Starting with the book of Moses, he begins to explain to them why the cross had to be. Gradually, he shows them that what had been causing them great sadness of heart, the death of the one they thought would rescue them from Roman imperialism, had actually been predicted centuries before as God's way of delivering them from a bondage far worse than political domination and oppression—the bondage of sin.

We have no record of the exposition given by Jesus on the Emmaus road that day. What did the Master say? Did he refer to Isaiah 53, where the servant who dies for sin in verses 1–9 appears alive and triumphant in verses 10–12? Did he focus their attention on Psalms 22, 23 and 24, and show them from those famous passages how the Messiah would come to the crown by way of the cross? We will never know: at least, not on this side of eternity. Doubtless the Master focused on many of the passages which pictured God's Messiah coming into the world to die, then rising again to validate his promises and usher in the kingdom of God. 'Ought not Christ to have suffered these things?' he said. In other words, 'Can't you see the fittingness of it all? Don't you see that it is the keystone of the arch?'

His exposition of the Scriptures no doubt kept them in a state of dawning comprehension and mounting excitement. So much so that when they reached their home, they pressed him to come in with them, share a simple meal and stay the night. As they sat down together, the Master asked God's blessing on the food, and as he took a small loaf of bread, broke it and passed it to them, their eyes were opened and they recognized who he was. Whether this recognition was triggered by seeing the nail-prints in his hands, or by some nuance in his voice, again we will never know, nor does it matter. Once they saw who he was, however, he vanished from their sight. In that moment of blinding revelation the matter of food was quickly forgotten. All they could think about as they looked at each other in astonishment was how their hearts had burned within them as the Master walked and talked with them on the road from Jerusalem to Emmaus.

What turned these two disconsolate travellers from sad, grief-stricken disciples into people whose hearts were on fire within them? Was it not the fact that Christ himself had been their teacher? Had he not revealed to them from his own lips the 'things concerning himself'? By the spoken word, and through the written word, they had seen the Living Word! Such an encounter cannot help but result in the experience of a burning heart.

Has something similar ever happened to you? Have you, at some time or other, opened the pages of your Bible in a somewhat discouraged or dejected mood, only to find, as you read, that the risen Christ comes alongside, floods the page with new and exciting meaning, at the same time mediating to you such an awareness of his presence that you come away with your heart burning within you?

The way to experience what the two travellers on the road to Emmaus described as a 'burning heart' is to meet Christ in the Scriptures, letting him minister to you the word of life until, in the process, your own heart bursts into flame.

How much time do you spend with the Bible? How much of your day (or week) is given to meditating in the word of God? 'The best kind of heartburn,' said a famous Welsh preacher, 'is *spiritual* heartburn,' and that comes only through spending time with Christ in the Scriptures.

Every Christian should plan to spend some time during each day quietly meditating in the Scriptures. It is here that we discover the truth about Jesus Christ, and as we peruse its pages, the Holy Spirit unfolds to us ever-increasing wonders concerning his Person. I know a devoted and sincere man who goes into his room each day and meditates on all the good and positive thoughts he can bring to mind. He believes he can get to God direct—without the need to come through Jesus and the Scriptures. But does he? I don't believe so. Talking to him, I found his concepts to be highly moral and wonderfully ethical, but he simply had no idea of who God is, and what he is *really* like. How can he unless he comes through God's self-appointed revelation—the Scriptures? This man believes that he can get to God through the medium of his own conceptions of God. His conceptions, in other words, are the medium. However, his conceptions of God are merely man's thoughts about God. The Bible, on the other hand, is God's revelation of himself. Unless human thoughts are constantly corrected by God's thoughts, then they are apt to go off at a tangent, so to speak, or simply mull around themselves. People who attempt to reach God through their own conceptions finish up self-centred, instead of Christ-centred—hence unsatisfied. They discover 'Christ within themselves' which turns out to be a Christ of their own creation. The lineaments of Jesus fade away and a Christ of sentimentalism takes his place. Then the description of the poet applies:

> They sail away on a sea of mist
> To a land that doesn't exist.

If Scripture is the centre, the circumference is everywhere. Once the revelation is fixed, then it can be unfolding. Pastor Robinson, one of the men who ministered to the Pilgrim Fathers, said, 'Much light will yet break out from the Word of God.' Christ has been revealing himself to his people through the Scriptures for close on two thousand years, and his revelations are inexhaustible. This book will be exhausted of meaning once it has been read through, but you can never exhaust the meaning in Jesus Christ. I love the way Moffatt translates Luke 1:78, 'Thanks to the tender mercy of our God, who will cause the Dawn to visit us from on high.' Those who come to the word of God expecting to find Jesus are living in a perpetual dawn. A surprise is around every corner. For Jesus, you see, is the centre of gravity of the Bible. He is the hub of the evangel. All the Old Testament truths converge on him, and all the New Testament truths emerge from him. When we recognize this—the fact that Christ lives in the pages of this thrilling book, the Bible—then life sparkles with novelty and with the dawning of new horizons.

'When Jesus stood up in the synagogue at Nazareth,' said one preacher, 'and read the passage from Isaiah which predicted his coming into the world (Lk 4:16–22), he proceeded to tell his hearers, "Today this scripture is fulfilled in your hearing." That day revelation passed from a law to a Life—from a book to a Person. Now that Person gives meaning to the book.'

How should we go about meeting the Person whose spirit resides within the precious volume we call the Bible? What are the attitudes we ought to adopt if we are to meet Christ in the Scriptures and come away with the experience of a burning heart?

Firstly, we must come to the Bible in a relaxed and receptive frame of mind. Psychologists tell us that we are only receptive when we are relaxed. 'Nothing,' they say, 'can be inscribed on a tense and anxious mind.' Start with the physical part of your being: let every muscle and every part of your body go limp. Next surrender all fears, all doubts and all inhibitions. Visualize Christ reaching out to touch your inner being. Invite him to minister especially to that part of your personality which is below consciousness. Spend a few minutes doing this before you

even open the Scriptures. Believe me, experience has
shown that it pays.

The pathway along which our Lord comes to the centre
of our beings is receptivity. It is as important as per-
ceptivity, for you only perceive as you receive. A
fourteen-year-old girl once told me of her plan for reading
the Scriptures. 'First,' she said, 'before even opening the
pages of the Bible, I sit quietly and empty my mind in the
Lord's presence. I give myself time to adjust to his world
of peace and tranquility. As I relax and let my body go
limp, I feel as if I am entering into a different world. I am
so happy.' She *was* in a different world—the invading
peace of God took hold of her entire being as she opened
up the centre of her being to God through relaxation and
receptivity.

This attitude says, 'Speak, Lord, thy servant heareth.'
Patience Strong says, 'If you go stamping through the
woods in a hurry, you will see and hear very little. But sit
still, and soon the squirrels come down the trees, the birds
will draw near, and nature comes alive in every twig and
tree and flower.' Once you are relaxed and receptive,
then nature becomes vocal. It is the same with the
Scriptures.

Secondly, we must come to the Bible with an eager and
expectant spirit. The Bible, it must be remembered, is
alive with hidden meaning. Speaking of itself, the Scripture
says, 'The word of God is living and active' (Heb 4:12,
NIV). A traveller tells of how, when crossing the Indian
Ocean on a liner, he saw two men begin their day in
different ways. One, a businessman, came down to
breakfast, picked up the newspaper and earnestly perused
its pages. Nothing, however, seemed to delight him, for
his repeated comment on the day's news was this, 'Just as
I expected.' Behind his back, the other passengers came
to refer to him as 'Mr Just-as-I expected'. His melancholy
spirit and gloomy disposition marked him out by the other

passengers as someone to be avoided. 'Another passenger,' said the traveller, 'began his day entirely differently. He would lean over the rail each morning, open up his Bible and was overheard to say to his wife, 'I wonder what the Lord has to say to us today?' When he finished reading, his face took on great calmness and strength.' He came to the word of God expecting God to speak some positive word of encouragement and hope, and he always appeared to get what he expected. If you come to the Bible in the same frame of mind, you too will be changed and transformed. Faith is expectancy—it stands alert and ready as the word of God is opened. So, 'according to your faith be it unto you.'

Thirdly, we must come to the Bible with the attitude that it is a moral and not a magical revelation. The practice of just opening the Bible anywhere and receiving the first words one reads as a personal, divine message has caused much harm. It would be wrong, of course, to suggest that God has never responded to such a method. John Wesley, for example, made occasional use of the Scriptures in this way: generally when he was overwrought, though he never used the method as a substitute for a close study of the Scriptures. One biographer reports that on the morning of 24th May 1738, he opened the New Testament at the words, 'Thou art not far from the kingdom of God.' At 8.45 p.m. that day the great experience came. This kind of thing, however, must be treated as exceptional. The Bible must not be treated like a lucky dip. Again I say, God will use his word in this way on certain occasions, but it must never be allowed to become a rule. The Bible must be studied—verse by verse—so that things can be kept in context. A good way is to read a book in one sitting, if possible, to get a general idea of the ground covered; then go back over the book, verse by verse, paragraph by paragraph. Don't be too hasty to finish a chapter. The deeper you get into the Bible the less you will need. F. W.

Faber said that a statement from the Scriptures which to a new Christian would seem tame and commonplace would satisfy a more mature saint for hours.

Fourthly, we must come to the Bible recognizing that the God who has spoken in the Scriptures speaks through it still. A famous missionary, when sharing with a group of Bible college students about his own personal approach to the Scriptures, said, 'Every time I read the Bible, before getting up and going about the business of the day, I ask myself these six questions: 1. Who is writing? 2. To whom? 3. What is he saying? 4. How does it apply to me? 5. How shall I put this into practice? 6. When do I begin?' He claimed that these questions, devoutly asked in the presence of God, made the Scriptures come alive to him day by day.

Such is the mystery of the Scriptures that as we question the record in the way described above, the divine Spirit will answer us, and God will use his word to speak to our need. Don't be concerned if the particular passage of Scripture you are studying does not contain the type of statements through which the voice of God can come direct to your soul. The saints down the ages have marvelled over the way that God takes familiar words, simple statements, and causes them to shine with a fresh light and with wondrous revelation. General statements, when touched by the Holy Spirit, come home with a personal application.

I remember, several years ago, passing through a serious personal crisis. My Scripture reading at that particular time was the systematic study of the first book of Chronicles. Quite frankly, I hardly expected God to speak to me out of a book that has largely to do with the history of ancient Israel. However, just one phrase of one verse stood out to me one day with such illumination and power that, under God, it became the means of solving my deep personal problem, and helped me to resolve the crisis. It is never enough to say that God has spoken through the Scriptures. He speaks through them still.

Fifthly, we must approach the Bible with a willingness to do everything our Master asks of us. Jesus once said, 'If any man will do his will, he shall know' (Jn 7:17). In a moral universe the key to knowledge is moral response. As we obey, so God reveals, but when we cease to obey then God shuts the book. For most of us, this is, I suspect, where our greatest problem lies. If we are honest we have to admit that our attitude toward the Scriptures is one of: 'Lord, show me how I can be happy, but at no great cost to myself.'

Dr L. W. Watkinson, a famous preacher of a bygone age, used to refer to the Bible as the 'mirror of Christ'. In one of his sermons he said, 'If we come to the Scriptures wanting simply something for ourselves, but not willing to see ourselves as we really are, then the *Mirror of Christ* will get steamed up by the hot breath of our selfishness. We will not see Him—and what is more, we will not see ourselves. And that is a tragedy of the highest magnitude.'

Once we are willing to follow through every challenge the Bible opens up to us, then the Scripture takes on a new power and comes across with new meaning. Permit me once again a personal illustration. I remember in the early days of my conversion being bound by a habit that caused me a good deal of personal distress. I wanted to give it up—and yet I clung to it with fierce determination. This ambivalence made my daily Bible reading an onerous task. Whenever I came to a passage that challenged me I would skip over it at speed until I found something less threatening and less demanding. I kept this up for weeks until I reached a point of serious emotional exhaustion. I realized that I was using up emotional energy to defend myself against the very word which could release me from my bondage and set me free. One morning, however, I opened the Bible, and never, as long as I live, shall I forget the transformation that took place in my life. As I approached the Scriptures, ready and willing to be challenged, the word cut like a rapier into my soul. Yes, of course, it hurt but, as the Africans say, 'It hurt good.' The Lord used his word, not only to reveal my inner condition, for the word that challenged me was the same word that healed me. From that day to this, I have learned the wisdom of approaching the word of God non-defensively. Now it is not so much me reading the Bible, but rather the Bible reading me.

Finally, we must come to the Bible to meditate on any truth that speaks to our spiritual need. If you find something that speaks to your condition, becomes authoritative, then roll it over and over in your mind. One of the reasons why people do not get the best out of the Bible is because they fail to meditate upon it. For some reason Bible meditation has been lost by the church of this century, and it desperately needs to be recovered. Some Christians are afraid of the word 'meditation' as it conjures up in their minds pictures of Indian gurus and eastern mystics. David Ray, an American writer and minister of the gospel, put it like this. 'I, for one, looked with suspicion on any Christian who advocated such a practice as meditation. I thought to myself: they are out of touch with reality. Give me action, lots of work. Let somebody else spend their days staring down the end of their nose.' Then someone introduced him to the art of Bible meditation. They showed him how to roll a thought around in his mind, extracting from it every drop of spiritual refreshment it contained. Within days, he claims, he became more aware of God's presence than ever before.

Meditation is not reading and memorizing the Bible or even studying the Bible. It is holding the word of God in your heart until it begins to affect every area and phase of your life. Meditation has been described as the digestive system of the soul. Rolling an appropriate biblical statement over in your mind will produce an atmosphere in your soul which will soon turn into an attitude—and then into an act. When Jesus was pressed by temptation in the wilderness, he answered, you will remember, with the words of Scripture. These words had become a part of him and, in the crisis, they naturally passed from the stage of assimilation and atmosphere to that of attitude and action.

One of the synonyms for the word 'meditation' is the word *ruminate*. Many animals, such as sheep, goats, cows, camels are called ruminant animals. This is because they have stomachs with several compartments—the first of which is called the rumen. The way a ruminant animal digests food is interesting. First, it literally bolts its food down. Then later it regurgitates the food out of its first stomach, the rumen, back into its mouth. This regurgitation system enables the food to be thoroughly digested, whereupon it is absorbed into the animal's bloodstream, thus becoming part of its life. Rumination and meditation, as I said, are synonymous. When a Christian takes a thought from the Scriptures and begins to meditate upon it, rolling it over and over in his mind and in his heart, the truth contained in that Scripture, whatever it may be, is absorbed in his spiritual bloodstream, producing spiritual power and energy in his being.

Meditation on the word of God, therefore, transmits the life of Christ which is in his word, the Bible, to every part of the Christian's personality. So remember, it is not enough simply to read the Bible, memorize the Bible or even study the Bible. To extract from it the life of God which is deposited in his word, we must meditate upon it. This, probably more than any other single thing, will result in us moving through life with a burning heart.

10

A heart filled with love

In the fifth chapter of Paul's epistle to the Romans, verse 5, we read these words: '... for we know how dearly God loves us, and we feel this warm love everywhere within us because God has given us the Holy Spirit to fill our hearts with his love' (TLB). This, then, is the subject on which we shall focus our attention in this final chapter—a heart *filled* with love.

Human definitions of love are far removed from those we find in the Scriptures. Ashley Montague, for example, in his book *The Meaning of Love*, starts out with the dictionary definition which reads: 'a feeling of deep regard, fondness, deep affection, usually accompanied by yearning or desire for; affection between persons of opposite sex, more or less founded on or combined with desire or passion.' In this definition, of course, we see the content of our contemporary society poured into the word.

Someone has said, 'If you want to witness the depravity of man—look into a dictionary.' Words associated with man become depraved by that association. The dictionary definition of love only very faintly reflects—if it reflects at all—the meaning of love as defined and described in the Scriptures. Obviously some parts of our language need to be redeemed. 'Love', in human terms, can mean anything from the sordid affairs of a film star or pop idol to the relationship which exists between two people of homosexual orientation.

In order to find the Christian content of the word 'love', we do best to examine two Greek words—*eros* and *agape*. In English they would both be translated as 'love', but the meaning is decidedly different.

The Greeks adopted the word *eros* to express their idea of love for God and man but the Christians adopted the word *agape*. The meaning the early Christians put into the word *agape* did not reflect its Greek source. It was adopted because it was the most expressive term available, but in its usage by those early believers, it became filled with a content that was distinctively Christian. And *agape*, when filled with Christian meaning, contains the most revolutionary idea ever to confront the mind of man.

'In ancient times,' said Dr E. Stanley Jones, 'two men commented about God. One was Plato who said, 'God is Eros.' The other was the apostle John who said, 'God is Agape.' Just the difference of two words—yet really there is between them the difference of two worlds.'

The New Testament never uses the word *eros* to define 'love', but consistently uses the word *agape*. What is the difference? The difference was never put more concisely than in the parallels given by Andrew Nygren:

Eros is acquisitive desire and longing; *agape* is sacrificial giving.

Eros is an upward movement; *agape* is a downward movement.

Eros is a man's way to God; *agape* is God's way to man.

Eros is man's effort; it assumes that man's salvation is his own work; *agape* is God's grace, the work of divine love.

Eros is egocentric love, a form of self-assertion of the highest, sublimest kind; *agape* is unselfish love, 'it seeketh not her own,' but delights to give itself away.

Eros seeks to gain its life, a life divine, immortalized; *agape* lives the life of God, therefore dares to lose it.

Eros is the will to get and possess, it depends on want and need; *agape* is freedom and giving which depends on wealth and plenty.

Eros is primarily man's love; God is the subject of *eros*. Even when it is attributed to God, *eros* is patterned on human love; *agape* is primarily God's love. God is *agape*. Even when it is attributed to man, *agape* is patterned on divine love.

Eros is determined by the quality, the beauty and worth, of its object; it is not spontaneous; it is evoked and motivated; *agape* is sovereign in relation to its object and is directed to both 'the evil and the good'; it is spontaneous, overflowing and unmotivated.

Eros recognizes value in its object—and loves it; *agape* loves—and *creates* value in its object.

As can readily be seen from this classic parallel of contrasts, *eros* is the raising of the human to the divine, the pursuit of egocentric religion; the other is the gracious condescension of the divine to the level of the human—the pursuit of the one true and living God. Here the issues are drawn. All systems and all life line themselves up on one side or the other. *Eros* is the love that loves for what it can get out of it. It turns everything—even God—into a means to its own end. *Eros* loves people for what they can give in return. If there is no return then love ceases. People who try to love God with an *eros* love are really saying to themselves, 'If I love God, then God will love me. And I will have the most wonderful thing in the world—the love of God for *me*.'

Another phase of this *eros* type of love is that when it is tied to religion it not only tries to make everything, even God, meet its own ends, it tries to get to God by its own means. And this is self-salvation. God, to the *eros* lover, is to be found at the end of a long climb up the ladder of salvation. The Almighty is met on his own level. God is attained by pure self-effort. Man has attained his own salvation. The Gnostics, a sect alive at the time of Jesus and during the life of the Early Church, believed that there were thirty-six steps by which a person could climb into perfect union with God. But Gnosticism was ego-centric and not Christ-centric.

In the Christian conception of love—*agape*—we do not find God at the topmost rung of the ladder but at the bottom. For we do not get to God—he comes to us, as in the Incarnation, and meets us on our own level. He reaches down to where we are in order to bring us up to where he is.

If, then, *eros* love is not the means by which we can know God, how do we go about replacing it with *agape*? Do we seek to cultivate it in our own strength? Can we produce it by an act of will? No, for the very effort we go to to produce it would make it a product of our self-attainment. and that would be *eros*—not *agape*.

Professor Hocking, in his *Human Nature and its Remaking,* says, '. . . The question "how is love to God or men possible if, in fact, I do not have it?" would be answered if there were, as the moving spirit of the world, an *Aggressive Lover* able and disposed to break in upon my temper of critical egotism and win my response [italics mine]. Read his words carefully again: 'An Aggressive Lover, able and disposed to break in upon my temper of critical egotism and win my response.' It is the good news of the Scriptures that the Aggressive Lover of whom Professor Hocking spoke is none other than God himself in the person of his Son, the Lord Jesus Christ. Saints down the ages have caught sight of that *Aggressive Lover*, and their own love has leaped out in flaming response, moving them to an intense love for God and man.

For centuries philosophers have despaired of the human race. With deep insight they have looked into the heart of man and claimed that he is so utterly selfish and egocentric that all hope of a new humanity is but an idle dream. 'Self-assertion and self-interest are so deeply ingrained in many,' they have said, 'that it is unchangeable and ineradicable.' Man is so made, they argue, that he is a prisoner of his own egotism, and nothing, simply nothing, can break the vicious circle of self-concern.

The Christian church, however, brings evidence to show how the circle of egotism may be broken, and how men and women may live out their lives on this earth with unconditional love. 'How,' we ask ourselves, 'is it possible for a human heart to be filled with a love that is unselfish, unconditional and divine?'

The answer hinges on the phrase found in John's first epistle: 'We love him, because he first loved us' (4:19). Put another way, it could read like this: 'His *agape* creates and inspires *agape* in us.' The source of this *agape* is God—hence pure. If the source of our love is in us it is bound to be *eros*—an acquisitive, self-centered love—hence impure. God is *agape*. That overflowing, spontaneous, unmotivated *agape* that flows from him creates an overflowing spontaneous and unmotivated *agape* in us. We love because he first loved us.

As a pastor and a counsellor for over thirty years, I have heard people, on innumerable occasions, say something like this: 'My problem is that I don't love God enough. How can I go about developing a greater love for him?' My usual reply to that question is this: 'No, that's not your problem. Your problem is that *you don't know how much God loves you.* When you see that then all your difficulties will vanish. Once we come to see that God is real and that he is love, then the scales drop from our eyes. As the blazing sun is set at the heart of the universe, and all things revolve around it, so the burning love of God is at the heart of all the life of the Spirit, and without it such life would be impossible.

How Christians come to an awareness of God's love for them varies, of course, with individuals, but the central place from which the revelation flows is the hill called

Calvary. There the heart of God is unveiled. It is the place of supreme revelation. Let us draw near once again to the cross, and with softened footsteps and hushed spirits, pause to worship and adore!

Gazing at the cross a number of things happen to us. In those five bleeding wounds, we see not just the agony of God but also his burning affection and love for lost sinners. We see there that we are loved with a love that has no strings attached. He does not love us if we will do this or that. He loves us for ourselves alone. Nothing in us gave rise to it and nothing in us can extinguish it. It is love without condition and without end.

Not being loved *for* anything, we know that no failure or imperfection in us can rob us of that love. It dawns upon us that we cannot even sin this love away. Sin produces a rift in the relationship between God and us, of course, but the cross spells out the message that sin is defeated, and, try as we will, we can never escape this Aggressive Lover. When we sin, his loving disciplines follow us until they track us down, turn us around to face the cross, and the sight of that bleeding, sagging figure of our Lord soon brings our souls out through our eyes in hot, adoring tears of repentance and love.

The more we reflect on the fact that God loves us and loves us unconditionally, the more we begin to realize that this love cannot be adequately explained. No man can or will ever explain why God loves us. If we could explain it then it would mean that God loves us for something outside of himself, not for ourselves alone. Charles Wesley expressed it this way:

He hath loved, He hath loved us
Because—he would love.

He chose to—just because he is love.

When we focus upon the fact that God loves us, and we perceive it for what it really is, unconditional and unselfish, then in the depths of our being that selfsame love is generated. It is not the fruit of labour, nor the effort of the flesh. Having seen the love of God, and seen it where it can be most clearly seen—at Calvary—the selfsame love is created in our hearts. Wonder breaks out and rapture swells in our soul until we feel like singing:

> 'Tis love! 'Tis love! Thou diedst for me!
> I hear Thy whisper in my heart;
> The morning breaks, the shadows flee,
> Pure, universal Love Thou art;
> To me, to all, Thy mercies move,
> Thy nature and Thy name is Love.

The late Dr W. E. Sangster, one of the great preachers of a past generation, in his book *The Pure in Heart,* said, 'Heaven knows no higher strategy for begetting love in mortal hearts than by bringing them to Calvary. There the scales fall from their eyes and they see. Seeing his love, their own love flames in response. To see that love, really see it, is enough. Not even sin can resist it. The heart plays truant and runs to its rightful Lord.'

One of the greatest needs in the Christian church these days is the need to focus on the fact that unless our love is derived from God's love, then our life of Christian service will be greatly hindered in its effectiveness. Many Christians set about serving their fellow men with an *eros* love, not an *agape* love. The love which God begets *in* us by the vision of his love *for* us is the love that we must share with all mankind. To share any other kind of love is less than the best.

How can we be sure it is *agape* and not *eros?* We can test it in all our relationships. We must ask ourselves: does it leave the recipient free? Is it love seeking to gain something from another, or is it love that gives because it delights to give? As we have seen, so much human love is love for something, even when we think it is the pure love of God. God alone knows how much evangelistic and missionary effort, ostensibly offered in Christ's name, has failed because it did not rest on the purity of *agape* love.

Many years ago I talked to a missionary in Nairobi, Kenya, who, after attending a seminar at which I had talked about the need for purity of motive, followed me to my hotel room and asked me for help. 'Tonight,' he said, 'I saw for the first time that my life as a missionary has largely been devoid of the pure love of God. I have come to the mission field at great personal sacrifice, having given up a lucrative job and career, but so much of my life has been motivated by *eros* and not *agape*. I have loved people in order to get them converted, rather than loving them for their sakes alone. Please help me to get this all straightened out—tonight.'

After about an hour of counselling, I knelt with him in the room and prayed that God might give him a new vision of the cross. Nothing happened for about half an hour, but then he suddenly began to weep and sob violently. After several minutes of this, he grew calm and composed. I asked him what was happening. 'I see the Lord Jesus Christ on the cross,' he said. 'He is looking at me with the most loving expression I have ever seen. His eyes are pouring out love. It is as if he is saying to me, "I gave my life for *you*, you. Not just a world of sinners lost—but you—personally."' Then, for about another half-hour, he stayed on his knees in complete silence. So great was the presence of God in the room that I also remained motionless. When our prayer time was over, my missionary friend stood up and said, 'Tonight, for the first time in my life, I have realized that before I am able to give love I must first be able to receive love. From now on

I am not going to try and convert people; I am going to let God love them through me.'

I heard from another friend in Kenya, who wrote to me some time afterwards, that the missionary returned to his duties a changed man. His friends couldn't believe the transformation in his life. One of the natives expressed it in these words: 'Before you seemed to have a love for us as big as this,' at which point he held his hands just two inches apart. 'But now,' he said, stretching his hands as wide as they would go, 'you seem to have a love as big as this.' The missionary (so I am told) said, 'There is only one place in the world where anyone can get a love as big as that—it's on a hill called Calvary, where a man called Jesus spread his arms as wide as they could go—and there, out of love, he bled and died for me.'

Just as God's love leaves any mortal free to accept or reject it (and continues, nevertheless, in its loving) so the love of one man for another, if it be *agape* love, is love without condition and love without bargaining.

What, then, is the answer to living a life of pure love? How can we be sure, as Paul bids us in the verse we considered at the beginning of this chapter, that our hearts are filled with love? The supernatural love that the Holy Spirit begets in the soul of a Christian is a love that loves God first! It is love without selfish interests and love without end. It is not for anything. It has insight, patience and asks nothing for itself—though, of course, it is gladdened by responsiveness. But it can wait, even for that.

This kind of love makes the world go round. It is the love which 'never fails'. May it fill your heart and mine—from here to eternity.